Confederate Currency
The Color of Money
Images of Slavery in Confederate and Southern States Currency

Confederate Currency
The Color of Money
Images of Slavery in Confederate and Southern States Currency

the paintings of **John W. Jones**

edited by **Gretchen Barbatsis**

contributions by

Gretchen Barbatsis
Richard Doty
Curtis Franks
Wilmot A. Fraser
Jack McCray
Donald West

Published in conjunction with the exhibition *Confederate Currency: The Color of Money, Depictions of Slavery in Confederate and Southern States Currency.*

Printed in China

Photography by Jack Alterman Studios, Inc.

To book lectures by John Jones, please visit www.colorsofmoney.com

ISBN 0-9722823-2-7 [cloth]
ISBN 0-9722823-1-9 [paper]

To all the descendants of slaves in the Diaspora

— JOHN W. JONES

SOUTH
5
CAROLINA
THE
PLANTERS BA
Will pay
FIVE D
on demand.
WINNS
FIVE
Cash.r

Confederate Currency
The Color of Money
Images of Slavery in Confederate and Southern States Currency

the paintings of **John W. Jones**

edited by **Gretchen Barbatsis**

Contents

Foreword

Curtis Franks

It is indeed a pleasure and a privilege for me to pen the introduction to this catalog, as a companion to John Jones' provocative exhibition *Confederate Currency: The Color of Money.*

I had the good fortune to serve as Curator during the infancy of this exhibit. Throughout the time the exhibition was at the Avery Museum, it provided scholars and the general public, particularly young people, an opportunity to gain additional insight and visual documentation of the pervasiveness of the institution of slavery. Moreover, the exhibition served as a virtual catalyst to formal and informal discussions on the institution of slavery and its continuing "currency" in debates and discussions relative to the conditions of people of African descent in America today.

Needless to say, the exhibition has a special resonance in the states that comprised the Confederacy. Given the fact that a number of southern states are engaged in never ending discourse relative to signs and symbols of the Confederacy, it is my hope that the exhibition will be seen in venues throughout the South during the next three years that it travels the country. More times than not, these discussions or arguments have been put forth as if the institution of slavery were not the foundation of the "Southern Way of Life." Moreover, this myopic view of the Confederacy has given additional life to perspectives that continue to divide communities, cities and states. In all likelihood these divisive debates will continue as long as the history of one ethnic group is celebrated and the history of another ethnic group is denigrated.

John W. Jones, a son of the South, has created a body of work that has the potential to serve as a vehicle for honest and candid discussion and debate of issues concerning race and class in American life. Furthermore, the exhibit lends itself to a re-examination of a very important period in American history– a period wherein lies the antecedents of the issues of race and ethniity. Through Jones' masterful execution of these wonderful works of art he has made a significant contribution and in the process he has provided us an opportunity to educate and re-educate ourselves about slavery and its continuing currency in American history.

In addition to illustrations of Jones' paintings and the accompanying Confederate and Southern notes, this catalog is comprised of five essays that "speak truth to power." The essays provide additional information and interpretation of Jones' work. In the words of Jack McCray, one of the contributors to this volume, all of the essays are "powerful riffs on the same theme."

Acknowledgments

A complex project such as *The Color of Money* would not be possible without the encouragement, sacrifice, support and talent of many individuals and organizations. I thank God for giving me the opportunity to tell this story through my acrylic on canvas paintings, and for bringing together people throughout the country to make this work a national success.

When I first presented the idea of this exhibition to Dr. Marvin Dulaney, Executive Director of the Avery Research Center for African American History and Culture in Charleston, South Carolina, he immediately saw its potential and proceeded to offer his personal support as well as that of the Avery Research Center. During that discussion, we came up with the name *Confederate Currency: The Color of Money, Depictions of Slavery in Confederate and Southern States Currency*. The successful showing at the Avery Museum (February – December, 2001) would not have been possible without the able support of its staff. I wish to thank Dr. Karen Chandler and Sherman Pyatt and especially Curtis Franks, the Director of Museum Education and Exhibitions at the Avery Museum and the curator of this exhibition. His expertise turned the project into an exhibition of national interest. I also want to thank Chuma and Barbara Nwokike and the staff of Gallery Chuma, Inc. in Charleston, South Carolina for bringing my artwork to the attention of the world. I am grateful to David Firestone of the *New York Times*, whose feature article brought the exhibition to a national limelight that has resulted in over 260 feature stories across the country.

All through this journey, I have been fortunate to meet outstanding individuals who have voluntarily offered their help and expertise. I wish to thank Dr. Betty Lovelace of Denison University who put me on the national lecture circuit. I also wish to thank Stanley Sneed, Chairman of the Board of Directors of The Institute for the Advanced Study of Black Family Life and Culture in Oakland, California for his foresight and perseverance in bringing the exhibition to the African American Museum and Library at Oakland, and I extend appreciation to the organizing committee, Dr. Wade Nobles, the Executive Director of The Institute for the Advanced Study of Black Family Life and Culture, Dr. Woody Carter, Executive Director of the Bay Area Black United Fund, Pat Patterson of Pat Patterson and Associates, who co-coordinated the exhibition as well as lectures and four town hall meetings. Thanks to Rick Moss, Chief Curator and Director of the African American Museum and Library at Oakland and Erica Watkins, Museum Curatorial Specialist, for the wonderful job in presenting the exhibition to the public.

My deepest appreciation and thanks also go to Dr. Gretchen Barbatsis for working so tirelessly in all aspects of this exhibition, from writing and design of the *Teacher and Docent Guide* to editing and design of the exhibition *Catalogue*. She became the center of gravity of this exhibition by using her professional expertise to bring needed balance and keep me focused on the story being told in the engravings of slavery on Confederate and Southern States Currency when I could easily have been diverted to the historical discussion of American slavery.

I wish to thank Joahne Penney of Kenosha, Wisconsin, for her love of this project. She became enchanted the moment she encountered these paintings and currencies and has worked tirelessly ever since to bring the exhibition to light.

I most gratefully acknowledge all my collectors for loaning the works to this exhibition, and whose patronage has made it possible for me to tackle this project. My special thanks to Dr. Harold Rhodes III, who has loaned twenty of the paintings in the exhibition. I am also grateful to the paper money collectors who have sent me copies of Confederate currency of which I had not been aware. I have to especially thank collectors Eric P. Newman and Will Bentley for sending me copies of rare issues.

It is my hope that other collectors will send me photocopies of currencies that are not yet depicted in this collection.

In concluding, I wish to thank my family for being my greatest supporters and for encouraging me right from early childhood when I first started painting. Thanks to my big brother Eddie, for helping with the exhibition.

—John W. Jones

Tour Schedule

Franklin G. Burroughs
Simeon B. Chapin Art Museum
Myrtle Beach, South Carolina 29577
August 17, 2006 - October 29, 2006

Federal Reserve Bank of Cleveland
Learning Center and Money Museum
Cleveland, Ohio
February 6 - April 20, 2006

The Augusta Museum of History
Augusta, Georgia
September 24, 2005 – November 1, 2005

The Siege Museum
City of Petersburg
Petersburg, Virginia
May 13 – July 31, 2005

Exhibition in conjunction with the
"African Americans and the Civil War" Conference at Virginia State University.

The Cochenour Gallery
Georgetown College
Georgetown, Kentucky 40324
March 7 - April 15, 2005

Exhibition in conjunction with the second Underground Railroad Summit
"Reframing History: African Americans in the Civil War"
March 31 - April 2, 2005

Milliken Gallery
Converse College
Spartanburg, South Carolina
January 8 – February 15, 2005

National Symposium, and an interdisciplinary course called "The Art and Economics of Race" was offered by two Converse Professors, in conjunction with the exhibition.

African American Atelier
Greensboro, North Carolina
October 10 - December 31, 2004

Rosa Parks Museum
Troy State University, Montgomery, Alabama
August 14 - September 30, 2004

St. Joseph's Historic Foundation, Inc.
July 12 – August 6, 2004
Durham, North Carolina

The Black World History Museum
St. Louis, Missouri
April 19 - June 30, 2004

Broward County Main Library
Gallery Six
Fort Lauderdale, Florida
February 7 - February 29, 2004

Schumacher Gallery
Capital University, Columbus Ohio
January 5 - January 31, 2004

Martin Luther King Jr. National Historic Site
Atlanta, Georgia
May 21 - December 15, 2003

Louisiana State University
Baton Rouge, LA
February 17 - April12, 2003

Rome Art & Community Center
Rome, New York
January 3 - January 31, 2003

Benedict College
Columbia, South Carolina
November 22 – December 18, 2002

America's Black Holocaust Museum
Milwaukee, Wisconsin
July 24, 2002 - November 6, 2002

African American Museum and Library at Oakland
Oakland, California
April 20 - June 29, 2002

Avery Research Center Museum
Charleston, South Carolina
February 2001 - December 2001

A Visual Storyteller Engages the Gap

Gretchen S. Barbatsis

I did not plan to visit the exhibition that is the subject of this essay, *Confederate Currency: The Color of Money*.[1] I didn't even know about it. I had gone to the Avery Research Center for African American History and Culture to hear an author speak about her book on the Gullah Geechie culture of Sapelo Island off the coast of Georgia. Because the reception and book signing were held in a gallery space, I found myself, wine in one hand and light hors d'oeuvres in another, viewing the paintings which hung around the room. The experience was anything but casual, however. In fact it seemed awkward. I felt confused and embarrassed.

Here I was, in the presence of images, such as "Slaves Picking Cotton," that seemed to be positive, if romanticized, depictions of slavery. The paintings were large and close-up in scale, the light was bright and natural, and the colors were bold and uncomplicated acrylics. Why, I wondered, would the Avery Research Center for African American History and Culture be presenting a picture of happy slaves— well dressed, healthy, smiling, and content to be a part of a brutal system that stole their labor.

"Slaves Picking Cotton"
Collection of Dr. Harold Rhodes

The presence of a happy, almost carefree image of a slave mother and child, presented in the painting "Slave Mother and Child," seemed particularly jarring in the context of an institution that routinely separated families and sold children. Here again the closely framed image was rendered with bright light and bold hues.

"Slave Mother and Child"
Collection of Sybil Y. Parson

An apparent disconnect between what these images were saying and the context in which they were saying it drew me to a much smaller image, elegantly matted in an ornate gold fame. I recognized it as an old piece of paper money, one issued in the South by a bank in Georgia. Discovering that a similar small frame accompanied each painting, I began to see that the meaning of the paintings was to be found in the juxtapositions— in the gaps of the 'not given' material between the painting and the money.

"Oh, that's it!" I found myself saying to myself. I recalled the title of the exhibition: *Confederate Currency: The Color of Money*. "That's what it means," I thought. "This exhibition is about an economic system built on the backs of slave labor." With this insight, the images of enslaved Africans— strong men and women along with their children toiling in the cotton fields, hefting the bales and delivering wagon loads of the South's most important commodity to market—took on a poignancy betrayed by happy scenes and smiling faces. The money-painting juxtapositions made it clear that these black men, women and children were part of a system of property and profit.

" Slave Profits"
Collection of Dr. Harold Rhodes

In the painting "Slave Profits," a classical mythical figure, Moneta the Roman Goddess of Money, made this statement without shame, as did the image in "Admiring Their Slaves," of a plantation owner and his wife appraising their property of land and human beings. Both are given the dominance of foreground over the toiling enslaved laborers behind them.

"Admiring Their Slaves"
Collection of Dr. Alan Rashford

Stories of Enslavement

This insight, while interesting and powerful, however, is only the beginning of the experience that this visual storyteller, artist John W. Jones, has in mind. The money-painting pairs present a juxtaposition that entices us to figure out what meaning is to be made of this relationship. Perhaps the insight happens when a viewer discovers that the ornately framed currencies are different from one another and he or she begins to examine them more closely. Or perhaps it happens, as it did with me, by overhearing another viewer say, "Look! The painting is on the money!" Either way, one is compelled to peruse these old pieces of money.

Moving into the world of the currencies transforms the experience of the exhibition from poignant to haunting. The paintings, one now realizes, are not just images of slave labor; they are intimations of human thought— reproductions of scenes engraved on the money. Finding these images on the currency of Southern states and the Confederacy thrusts us into a world of people actively affirming and aggressively promoting the slave labor system of their plantation economy. This is a story of enslavement.

Now we are no longer engaged with the abstractions of paintings and money. Instead, the artist has created a juxtaposition of voice. On the one hand, by enlarging the engraver's images his paintings direct us to consider that a story is being told. The engravings tell a story of "the Southern way of life," affirming a natural relationship between benevolent owners and happy slaves in servitude to them. It's legitimacy is taken for granted in the context of national and mythical symbols which include George Washington, himself a slave owner, and the American flag, as well as classical objects and figures which also appear on the notes.

At the same time, by zooming-in to enlarge his subjects, as one sees with the painting "Slave Carrying Cotton," the artist thrusts these men, women and children into our space, releasing them from their bondage on the money and empowering them with direct address. While the currencies circumscribe their lives, the paintings set them free, and while it is the voice of enslavers that we find in the engravings, it is the voice of the enslaved Africans that we encounter in the paintings.

"Slave Carrying Cotton"
Collection of Dr. Harold Rhodes

What the artist found in painting these vignettes was, in his words, "the strong and indomitable character of the slaves, the will to survive and carry on the qualities they brought with them from Africa in the form of music, religion, storytelling, art, architecture, agriculture and culinary traditions." Though he presents the content as originally portrayed on the currencies without revision, through the use of scale, light, color and visual direct address he gives voice to the enslaved and, in doing this, creates a contending subject position from which to see and experience this 'Southern way of life.' While the engravings tell a story of enslavement, the paintings tell a story of empowerment.

Story of Empowerment

The story of empowerment told by the paintings begins with the artist's use of scale. By providing us with close-up images of the scenes of slavery that are engraved on the currencies, he moves the frame from vignette to storyworld. Within this frame we encounter not the iconic symbols of an economic system, but people with a story to tell. Through the creation of this space they are given voice.

The story of empowerment continues with the artist's use of color. He brings life to the monochrome engravings with highly saturated hues. The colors are primary, bold and uncomplicated: red, orange, yellow, green, blue, and violet.

His use of color portrays the nobility of his ancestors and of their work. They wear clothing in the ruby, emerald, amethyst, sapphire, pearl and gold of precious jewels. As we see in "Overseer with Whip," they toil under the red ochre of the midday sun, "an expansive hell," as Wilmont Fraser says, which overwhelms the entire cotton field. As he further describes, yellow ocher tones in the sky of "Mississippi Slave" and "Slave Family Picking Cotton," remind us of the gold they produce, and of their toiling from the 'can't see to can't see' half-light of dawn to dusk. And, a pervasive use of blues references, through indigo— another cash crop brought about by the knowledge Africans carried with them on the slave ships— a proud and noble heritage. Given the suffering endured by enslavement, this use of indigo also suggests the origin of the blues. Spirituals spoke of resistance and freedom and in this image a cool blue haze— the upward reflection of the sun's rays reversed by the white field of cotton— protects enslaved workers from the heat.[2]

" Mississippi Slave"
Collection of Nathalie Dupree

The story of empowerment is also told in the artist's use of light. The scenes are brightly lit, full of hope and faith. Despair is not an element of these stories. High angle lighting in many images adds a hint of spirituality.

Finally, through the use of close-up framing in juxtaposition to the wide field of view presented by the currency, the artist accomplishes the pictorial equivalent of a zoom-in. Without the painting, we might move into the aesthetic space of the engraving to engage this storyworld. This, being the equivalent of a dolly-in, would lock us in the contextual space defined by the currency and the voice of the engraver exercising his power to control the subjects' engagement in their own picturing.[3] The effect of the zoom-in, however, is to thrust the subjects into our space, and, as we experience with "Georgia Slaves" or "Slave Boy," for example, to empower them with the voice of direct address.

"Georgia Slaves"
Collection of Al Miller

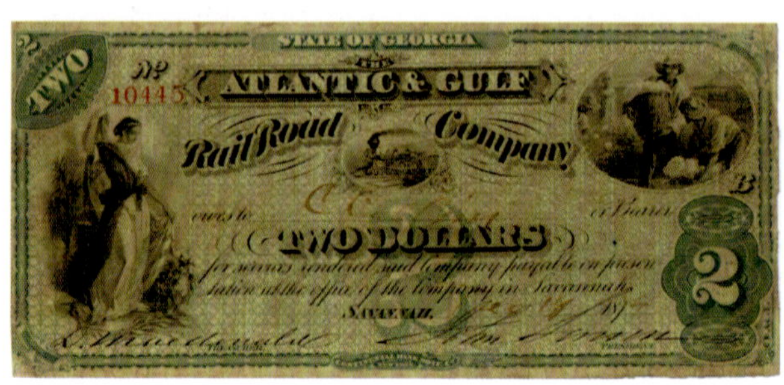

Story of Confrontation

By empowering his subjects with the voice of direct address, the artist engages us in yet another story, one which compels us to confront the persistent meaning of a system which enslaved. This is a story of confrontation. In a relationship of direct address with the subjects in the paintings, we become participants in their storytelling. Taking this subject position, we are in a posture to see the engraved slave vignettes reflexively. In juxtaposition to the engravings, the paintings reveal the presence of a voice engaged in the activity of 'othering.' We recognize the engraver's power to compel his subjects' complicity with their observer. It is as if those who address us through the paintings challenge us to engage the phenomenon of their 'othering.' Through this maneuver, of giving his subjects voice and then using it to reveal how it was taken from them, the artist cleverly and subtly entangles us in their pain. He makes us experience what was taken from them.

Looking again at the artist's rendering of Moneta, the Roman Goddess of Money in the painting "Slave Profits," we can see how the artist uses color to reinforce this experience. He paints her as a mulatto, symbolizing the sexual as well as economic, political and socio-cultural exploitation of the slaveocracy that is shamelessly celebrated on its currency.

Once we have taken her subject position, it is unlikely that the piece of the historical puzzle called slavery will ever fit into the picture again. The currencies alone, ornately framed or not, tell the story of an inhumane and failed economic system, but they are easily relegated to the past. Even the paintings alone, while empowering their subjects with a sense of nobility, similarly allow us to put the story on the wall of history, a regrettable period, but one gone by. Their juxtaposition, however, subtly compels us to confront the living legacy of this experience. Through this visual storytelling structure, where the past is both background and foreground to the present, the artist creates a compounding point of view that will not allow us to contain the meaning of slavery as a story of the past.

NOTES

[1] More information on the exhibition Confederate Currency: The Color of Money is available on line at: http://www.colorsofmoney.com

[2] This analysis of color is indebted to a longer discussion in Al Fraser's essay "John W. Jones: Studying and Painting Blood Money in the New Millennium."

[3] For this experience you might visit the exhibition Beyond Face Value. It includes full color reproductions of 76 bank notes produced in slave and former slave states between the 1840's and 1880's. It is on line at: http://www.cwc.lsu.edu/cwc

" Slave Boy"
Collection of Ronald O. and Mittie R. Smith

Studying and Painting 'Blood Money' in the New Millennium

Dr. Al Fraser

Until this highly noteworthy exhibition, deep psychological inhibitions in African Americans may have precluded our studying the relationship between Confederate currency and our history. It seemed better to ignore the *blood money*, associated with the Confederate flag, with all the revulsions of slavery. Few experts in African American history, (if any) knew that engravings of African Americans on Confederate currency existed. Artistically, time's passage into the new millennium may have allayed such embarrassing unproductive sentiment and brought about a new awareness, of how heavily slavery endowed the Confederacy and the United States.

African American artist-illustrator, John W. Jones, after discovering numerous and surprising depictions of slavery printed on Confederate bills, has very skillfully recreated, magnified and expressively painted them, rendering a clearer quite dispassionate view of the bygone slave era; past in one sense, painfully persistent in others. Jones' work, *Confederate Currency: The Color of Money,* gives viewers the impression of events having come full circle. In these paintings, history informs art, which in turn artfully reveals more history. A new understanding arises from this synergy presaging a time of reckoning for the great contribution of blacks to America.

The whole exhibition sometimes obscures the most striking images of this collection of acrylic on canvas paintings. It is a visual flood of memorable images, including the corresponding Confederate currency. Wherever Jones' artist-illustrator, one-two punch hits hardest, however, the best paintings emerge from the series. The collection could eventually number many more works as even more bills depicting slaves circulated before the Civil War in the former Confederate States. Jones intends to paint each one as homage to his ancestors .

His skill as an illustrator able to render significant detail, enlivens the mostly mundane activities occupying the slaves in the original engravings where they were portrayed planting, chopping, picking, and transporting cotton, corn, sugarcane and tobacco. Slaves were also depicted catering food, making barrels, loading ships, grinding tools, butchering hogs and tending machines in factories, testifying cumulatively to a major economic dynamic. Jones says pointedly:

> *Cotton and slaves were the foundations on which the economy of the South was built. Cultures tend to put on their money what was important to them. Slavery was important to the South because it was on their money. You can use that little cliché... It's right on the money.*

Artistic ingenuity further develops the tiny monochrome engravings into magnificent expressive colorful paintings. Scenes that evoke questions about slavery, imbuing the people and the surroundings depicted with power and meaning, transmute the artist into a visual griot. "I didn't know they had slaves on the currency, that's what intrigued me about it" says Jones. "It's almost like one of the best kept secrets. The stuff on the bills was so small, unless you were looking for it, you'd miss it."

> *When I paint these vignettes, I see the strong and indomitable character of the slaves, the will to survive and carry on the qualities they brought with them from Africa in the form of music, religion, storytelling, art, architecture, agriculture and culinary traditions. My hope is that these paintings will allow viewers to reflect on the issues of slavery as it relates to race relations, in an atmosphere free of censorship.*

A pairing of each painting in the exhibition with the framed Confederate currency or Southern bank note from which it derives, provides a means of checking the faithfulness of the artist's acrylic rendition against the original engraving. Since the

"Slave Overseer with Whip"
Collection of Dr. Harold Rhodes III

Confederate images often were idealized, even romanticized, the bill's presence is essential to understanding the true origins of these vignettes; otherwise one might walk away with a reinforced belief in the depictions of "happy slaves." Jones observes,

> *They were important properties displayed on their paper money, showing the slaves as happy, well treated and healthy workers in an "unnatural" state of bliss... you never see anything with any hardships like slaves being whipped or something like that. It's always happy, most of them are just happy picking cotton,*

While there may be room for much mischief should the paintings become separated from the currency– an impossibility were these the works of a modern collagist– Jones is a very talented realist.

Faced with the dilemma of "how to make picking cotton seem exciting," Jones decided to "present the engravings as originally portrayed on the currencies without revision," but to use "colorful acrylics on canvas to bring the paintings back to life and capture the viewers interest long enough to confront the difficult subject of slavery."

The artist's powers of observation, draftsmanship, and colorful expression became crucial in extracting from the dehumanized engravings the essential humanity of their subject matter, not to just render but to celebrate this quality."Striving for detail in light and reflection, I meticulously draw each painting first, and then layer it with color, resulting in very real interpretations of everyday life and landscapes, as well as historical insights into our past," says Jones in summarizing his painting process.

Still one must actually witness the transition from the monochrome engraving to Jones' color painting, In "Slave Overseer with Whip" the artist employs red ochre to convey mood; the midday sky, an expansive hell, violently overwhelms the entire cotton field, where slave pickers toil and apparently broil, while the slave overseer with whip, in broad hat, looks down from horseback.

Down low in the cotton, Jones paints a cool blue haze, the upward reflection of the sun's rays, reversed by the white field of cotton, that protects the slaves from the heat, and demonstrates the artist's mastery of his subject matter and technique. Yellow ochre tones symbolize money. The color-coded yellow sky appears again in the half-light of dusk or dawn in "Slave Family Picking Cotton," rendering real the old slave cliché "from can't see, to can't see." The sight of this entire family enslaved forms a telling indictment of the system.

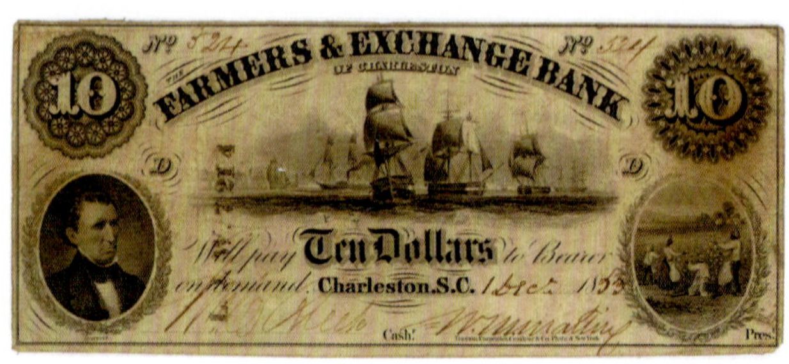

"Slave Family Picking Cotton"
Collection of Dr. Jack Bass

"Slave Sowing Seed"
Collection of Dr. Al Fraser

In "Slave Sowing Seed" blue pigments capture the forlorn mood and predicament of a young slave man barefooted and in tattered clothing, reluctantly at work planting cotton and unable to reap what he has sown. Trapped in slave status, hard at work, his suffering interprets visually into the origins of the blues. Here Jones selects indigo, another African derived slave produced cash crop, to color and reveal American history.

Another historical message is color-coded in red, white and blue in the painting "Slaves Unloading Cotton" where Jones' tri-colored sky exposes how, in an image from an antebellum Alabama bank note, an engraver connects slavery, the U.S. flag, and the country's fledging transportation industry.

"Slaves Unloading Cotton"
Collection of Alphonso Brown

One notes that the U.S. Government, not just the South, benefited from slavery and supported the institution– in the Fugitive Slave Act and many other repressive laws as well as in the Constitution itself (Article 1, Sec. 9) from the nation's beginnings until the Civil War.

"Slave Profits"
Collection of Dr. Harold Rhodes III

Perhaps the most striking image of the entire exhibition, "Slave Profits" depicts the Roman goddess of money, Moneta, painted with artistic license as a mulatto, a symbol of the sexual and general exploitation of the enslaved caste. Jones displays here and throughout the series, his special ability to accurately render the varied skin tones and physiognomies of African Americans. Moneta sits blue robed, blonde haired, holding in one hand a cotton branch with four bolls, and squeezing a sack full of gold coins in the crook of her other arm. Spilling out at her feet are golden coins from another overflowing money sack. Behind her a cotton field filled with dark slaves and a white overseer on horseback awaits a railroad train approaching from the distance to collect the slaves' production. This allegorical painting exposes the direct exploitative relationship between racism, slavery, wealth and industrialization posited on the $5.00 bill issued by the Georgia Savings Bank in 1863. Because it originates from the culprit's own hand, the artist's indictment appears undeniable.

Can this exhibition of paintings extracted from old "slavery time" currency affect us much today? Viewers of the exhibit, black and white alike, have reacted with astonishment at the historic importance of African American slave labor to the economic development of the South and the United States depicted in the paintings. This new level of public understanding generated by exposure to Jones' slave paintings will help determine the outcome of important current issues related to African Americans, and crucial to the future development of American society. The paintings help to create a more enlightened public opinion on the much debated question of whether the United States owes and should pay reparations to African Americans for centuries of past slavery and racial discrimination that have unjustly benefited and prospered the nation.

"Slaves Loading Ship I"
Collection of Dr. Louis Hassell

Current issues suggested by these paintings of daily life during slavery include halting such everyday covert discrimination as voter fraud, police brutality and higher incarceration rates for blacks that threaten re-enslavement based upon hostile and differential treatment under the law.

"Slaves Loading Ship II"
Collection of The Rev. Dr. Wayne D. Pokorny

A majority African American longshoremen's union in Charleston, South Carolina recently had several of its members, "The Charleston 5," jailed after a labor protest that erupted in a violent confrontation with the police. Though the legal charges subsequently were resolved by uncontested pleas, this union can successfully mark its resolute refusal to regress to the days depicted in "Slaves Loading

"First Image"
Collection of Dr. Al Fraser

Ship I" and "Slaves Loading Ship II," when slave labor handled all cargo on ships in Charleston harbor.

Reactionary efforts to turn back the clock and rehabilitate the Confederacy confront us: flying the Confederate flag in public places at state expense; filling public library shelves with works proclaiming that "The South was Right" or that slavery never existed, except as "myth;" reasserting that the War Between the States (read Civil War) was fought for states rights and southern nationalism, not for slavery; recruiting a small cadre of misguided blacks to support these ideological views. These futile actions based upon psychological warfare tactics aim to propagandize the world into renewed acceptance of the discredited premises on which the defunct Confederacy was built: egotism, racism, selfishness and greed. Ironically, without the preservation of Confederate currency, this story would have remained undiscovered. But a contextual difference exists between Confederate chauvinism and legitimate historical preservation.

The paintings in this collection exhibit no bitterness. Considering their origins, they appear quite appropriately dispassionate. The exhibit gains its power from the multitude of memorable images of slaves, however humble, minds set on freedom, working for America, *for free*. They present a superb revelation in art of the many and multifarious contributions of African Americans to the economy of the South and the United States during slavery.

An intriguing conclusion arises from the images when one compares the portrayals of African Americans in the engravings, as they change over time. African Americans moved from being portrayed as equals working alongside whites and Indians to the subservient position of personal chattel, forced to labor under the whip, owned and overseen by whites. This depiction of the little understood transition that African Americans underwent when they first entered the American colonies as indentured servants and then over time were bound by the passage of restrictive laws into slavery or eternal servitude alerts us to be vigilant. Vigilance against restrictive legislation even in a dangerous era of terrorism remains crucial today to preserving African Americans' basic freedoms.

However well meaning, do these paintings about slavery implicitly beautify, glorify, justify or ratify, as did the original engravings, the evil institution of slavery? No more than the singing of spirituals in dialect. On the contrary, the paintings inform us about the resilience of our African American ancestors and how, despite supposed powerlessness, they overcame slavery: through undying faith in God and nature, persistent mentally and physically strengthening hard work, constant development of their individual talents and skills, and a spirit of cooperation even with whites, to attain mutual goals. We are also inspired to restore collective uplift through human creativity.

Expressed in the arts and culture, this energizing prescription is much like Kwanzaa principles practiced daily rather than being annually proclaimed.

In the new millennium John W. Jones' paintings clarify our view of slavery, and inspire us with scholarly vigor, craft, artistic creativity, beauty and truth. Like John, the trickster of slave legend, Jones has taken the old currency of the Confederacy and transmogrified it– economically and philosophically– into new money. Black and white collectors have acquired these paintings inspired by "Ol' Marster's" Confederate currency at prices ranging from $1550 to $6500 apiece.

Fortunately, these paintings tell a story that is right on the money, revealing for our era much more about America's history of slavery, and boldly prescribing the right medicine of recompense for the future. This exhibition should travel to Washington, DC so that Government officials may view its many scenes from slavery. If anyone needs a visual smoking gun proving how much and how variously slavery enriched America at the expense of African Americans, whose descendants today demand and rightly deserve long promised reparations, John Jones' genre paintings exerpted from Confederate currency provide a plethora of artful, historical and very convincing evidence of America's great debt to its former slaves.

A Look Through the Window of America's Soul

Signifying on American Cultural Images

Jack McCray

In a 1969 homage to Duke Ellington, Ralph Ellison included the great artist's response to being denied the Pulitzer Prize for music, ostensibly because of race. Ellington's now famous quote was, "Fate is being kind to me. Fate doesn't want me to be too famous too young. Ellison wrote of the quote:

> *"a quip as mocking of our double standards, hypocrisies, and pretensions as the dancing of those slaves who, looking through the windows of a plantation manor house from the yard, imitated the steps so gravely performed by their masters within and then added to them their own special flair, burlesquing the white folks and then going on to force the steps into a choreography uniquely their own.*
>
> *"The whites, looking out at the activity in the yard, thought that they were being flattered by imitation and were amused at the incongruity of tattered blacks dancing courtly steps, while missing completely the fact that before their eyes a European cultural form was becoming Americanized, undergoing a metamorphosis through the mocking activity of a people partially sprung from Africa.*
>
> *"So, blissfully unaware, the whites laughed while the blacks danced out their mocking reply."*[1]

Ellington (1899-1974) was in a tradition that now includes artist John W. Jones.

One day in 1997, Jones looked through a window himself, a magnifying glass in his case, not the window in the manor house. He didn't see nineteenth century white people dancing, as Ellison described; but he saw enslaved Africans pictured on the piece of Confederate currency brought into the blueprint shop where he was employed. The caller wanted the bill enlarged. Quickly after peering through the looking glass, things got more and more curious to Jones. What he saw stunned and excited him. There was an image of an African American woman, a slave, in a fantasy world of happy workers. This discovery piqued Jones' existing interest in history, so he began to do some research into Confederate money, which led to his finding out that putting images of enslaved Africans on currency was widespread in the South during the mid-nineteenth century on through Reconstruction.

As a result, we have Jones' series of fine art renderings of the engravings, *Confederate Currency: The Color of Money*. His act of painting these images is an exemplar of the creative process African Americans have indelibly stamped on American culture. He has stylishly recreated an object he saw by interpreting it, based on his own experience, and transforming it, in terms of meaning, to a level that transcends its initial purpose, thus ennobling himself, those who encounter the artifact, as well as the artifact itself.

This improvisational approach to solving the question, "Who am I?" is what's at the basis of the African American view of creativity, and, by extension, the American view.[2] The process of creating the artifact is a psychic journey down the road of self-discovery. The artifact, then, is a statement of self definition. The meaning at the core of the representation is the message the art brings. The message— affective, cognitive, and spiritual—of good art resonates with the observer. *Confederate Currency: The Color of Money* vibrates with its messages. Jones' artistic walk down the road to self-illumination brightens everyday life for those who view these paintings.

Also within the African American tradition, the artist seeks to express the universal in the particular, elevate the mundane and ordinary to elegance, and seek the sublime in the ridiculous, which the art of painting is eminently suitable to demonstrate. Singer Kurt Elling, a German-American and Chicago, Illinois resident, gave an example before a performance in Spoleto Festival USA in

Charleston, South Carolina in 2000 when explaining why he kept his engagement at the height of the NAACP boycott of the state over its flying of the Confederate flag. He believed that if Duke Ellington were confronted with the same situation, he would have wrapped himself in the Confederate flag on stage, given the best performance of his life, achieved a spiritual connection with the audience— in spite of the symbolic obstacles the flag represented— and rendered it powerless and meaningless in the face of transcendent art.

Like Ellington figuratively wrapping himself in the flag, Jones immersed himself in history and his artwork to produce oil paintings that are bold in style and substance. Visual contradictions abound. The benign, pastoral scenes (portrayed by one who grew up in similar settings) soar off the canvas in absolute stark visual contrast to the horrors of slavery felt in the heart. The bright colors seem to pound home the message. As one views the paintings, the connection comes in waves. Like Jones before 1997, most people have never seen slave images on Confederate money, so upon viewing the exhibit, we learn something. We have new information, and it affects how we feel. After the galling feeling that comes from realizing Confederates had the temerity to do this subsides, Jones' interpretations impart the ultimate grace-under-fire lived by enslaved Africans in America. Jones' love for these figures comes beaming through in the paintings. It comes on the same energy wave that tells the viewer these enslaved Africans lived with dignity and respect against all the odds. The paintings also have a blues flavor that flows into the viewer's consciousness when looking at them, and remains there with a bittersweet aftertaste.

Jones' family hails from rural Fairfield County in South Carolina. He grew up around farming, and to this day, travels the back roads of South Carolina, immersing himself in that ambience and providing himself with intuitive materials with which to inform his art—much like Edwin Harleston (1882-1931), an African American Charlestonian who painted local scenes and people in the early twentieth century. He remembers his paternal great-grandmother, a former slave who died at the age of 109 in 1967. She still had the scars from whippings on her body.

Until the African American way, manifested mostly through music and literature, became the American way, this country's art was an attempt to force American themes into European forms. Art, dance, music, and literature in the United States tried to make this country a European one in the Western Hemisphere. Genre painting (local, everyday scenes) popular here in the nineteenth century is an example of this phenomenon.

As a solid American identity emerged in the early twentieth century— following defeats of England in 1812, Mexico in 1848, and Spain in 1898, and the wresting of industrial leadership of the world from England— what differentiated this country from those in Europe was what Africans brought here and used to "jazz" up the culture.
Sports, storytelling, agriculture, food, and practically everything else in this country, has been heavily influenced by the African cornerstone used to build American culture. The influence sits squarely in the bedrock of this culture.

In addition to its African influence, the American approach to art is based in large part on the notion or idea of democracy. This is the first effort in the history of the planet to form a government by consent of the governed with the highest respect given to individual rights and the freedom to make choices. This tradition allows us to change directions and reinvent ourselves— all while everybody else is doing the same thing. So, we try things and fail; we bump into others in their pursuit of happiness as we chase it ourselves; we encounter obstacles all day, everyday, large and small; unpredictable things happen causing sudden turns in direction; we go fast, we go slow; we're happy, and we're sad. We get the blues. That's why the blues is plural, not singular. There are a ton of ways to get them and a never-ending number of ways to chase them. We know they're going to come, so in order to deal with them on our own terms, we invite (subconsciously most of the time) the blues so we can stomp them.

Ironically, African Americans have had the least freedom of all American immigrant groups. Despite the inability to navigate society as freely as everyone else, however, African Americans have taken the blues aesthetic to profound depths, having the largest and most frequently occurring dragons to slay, but approaching heroic dimensions while wonderfully wielding the improvisational sword against large and small nemeses. Jones' brush is his sword.

Blacks aren't good at the blues only because they're sad and were once slaves missing their homeland. They brought from Africa a distillation of thousands of years of civilization that included an innate ability to perceive their situation and come up with a strategy that allowed them not only to survive, but also to change their surroundings.[3] Many whites couldn't see through this window until after the Civil War because of the cultural curtains African Americans had hung.

Much is made of the North outnumbering the South, blacks joining the war on the side of the North and northern industrial superiority as the reasons the North won. A most significant factor, too, was the general work stoppage and sabotage by enslaved Africans.[4]

The antebellum days had many whites believing blacks were actually docile, happy, and glad to relinquish the fruits of their labor and technological skills to their masters— just as they're pictured on Confederate currency. They not only feigned that persona to survive, but underneath the mocking obsequiousness was a subtle strike back that bought time, allowed for the honing of retaliatory skills, and lulled the enemy into a cultural deep sleep that they didn't awaken from until it was too late.

This African worldview was most pronounced in the Gullahs, most of whom were in South Carolina, Jones' home state. The planter princes and their descendants who held sway through the war brought Africans in from practically the entire western coast of Africa, particularly the Rice Coast, to engineer, plant, and harvest the golden rice fields, among other labors.[5] Gullahs were already improvising life when they got here. The movement of people in Africa had families, tribes, and nation states intermingling, at least culturally, adapting to new circumstances, and making the most out of whatever situation they found themselves in.[6]

A part of the prevalent nothing-happened-until-slavery theory about blacks is that Africans were one, homogeneous, monolithic group before coming here, just as they were after arrival and continue to be. In the traditional African worldview, everything has practical applications. Art for art's sake hasn't much of a place in African cultural values, and Jones' first reaction to slave images on currency wasn't artistic. It was a blues kind of feeling, sour then sweet. There was astonishment, and later a gut feeling that became a cognitive sighting. It made him angry, but more importantly, it provided unequivocal proof that the Civil War was fought over slavery, a premise vehemently denied to this day by many Confederate supporters and revisionists.

Confederate Currency: The Color of Money is not art for art's sake. Technique is important to the extent that it provides a vehicle for its message and a comfortable conveyance for the messenger, the artist. It's meant to be seen and experienced so that the viewer may learn something and be moved. A part of Jones' conception with this series was to complete a segment of an extended work he mounted years ago. He has set out to depict the history of Africans in America. The murals Aaron Douglas (1898-1979) painted, (with significant help from Harleston at Fisk University in Nashville in 1930) during the Harlem Renaissance come to mind. Most of his considerable work before this series has to do with black life. Slave images on Confederate money reveal and confirm that not only was the African American creative process underneath the American one, black images also provided the content.

About the same time banks started issuing these notes, Theodore D. Rice went up on a stage in New York City in 1833 with burnt cork on his face to entertain an audience. He took the stage name Jim Crow, named after a dance he dubbed "Jump Jim Crow." His entertainment was to jump and flail about, singing ditties and making base, grotesque gestures and sounds, all mimicking what he saw when Negroes entertained themselves and whites. A genre painting by an unidentified artist depicting the scene exists in the Museum of the City of New York Theater Collection.[7]

Unlike the refined, European-like dancers in the manor house, Jumpin' Jim Crow was outside doing the most unrefined things. Unlike the blacks' improvisation on the manor house dancers—artistically transcendent, technically proficient, and uplifting— Jim Crow's take on the blacks he saw dancing in a slave cabin was a garrish, malevolent, racist caricature that fed the psychoses from which he and those like him were evidently suffering. American popular culture had been born.

With the release in 1848 of Stephen Foster's "Oh Susannah!" the American popular song appeared by its first celebrated song writer, who provided a formula which has a variation still in practice today in the marketplace of culture—whites imitating blacks. Paul Whiteman did it in the Jazz Age, Benny Goodman in the Swing Era and Elvis Presley in the post-modern, Rock and Roll Age. Eminem rules the Hip Hop Age.

Minstrelsy took off like a rocket. It was a hit around the world. Before then, not much attention had been paid in other countries to anything cultural coming out of the United States.

American literature didn't begin to get any attention until many decades later, as did art and sculpture. Other significant American contributions, such as the movies and architecture, didn't have their impact until the 20th century.

This is the culture in which the decisions were made to use black images on currency. The image of the benign, subservient slave worked just fine for those in control of the economy, and they—South and North— went to work making all the money they could on the backs of blacks—literally and figuratively. This demeaning visual image huckstering didn't fade considerably until the middle of the twentieth century. As the Industrial Age barreled along, national transportation emerged, and the middle class grew, Americans bought more and more of the goods they used to make. So advertising grew to a national level, spawning the "Aunt Jemimas" and the "Uncle Bens." Docile, stereotypical blacks were like mascots, warm and fuzzy, so images appeared on everything from patent medicine to chewing tobacco. Technological change had made the reproduction of these visual images easier and cheaper. Asian and Native American images were also exploited, but none compared to the exploitation of the African American image. After Reconstruction, images such as these went on to be used to make and justify the culture of segregation, whose late nineteenth century, early twentieth century manifestation came to be known as the Jim Crow Era.

Images promulgated by minstrelsy made it okay to live by apartheid. It soothed the souls of those who maintained the system to pronounce that though inferior, blacks would be the recipients of their largesse through a separate-but-equal policy in running the government and allocation of resources. Race had become the way to organize and order the post Civil War United States. The only thing all whites agreed on was that blacks should be at the bottom of the ladder, freedom from chattel slavery notwithstanding. Former Confederates, beleaguered farmers, a working class growing larger, western settlers, women's rights advocates, the Northeastern elite, and a more powerful scientific community, all used race to establish new self identities.[8]

Ironically, in the 1950s and 1960s, white images would be used to sell black music to white people. Major record labels packaged black rock and roll in record jackets with white people pictured on them.

The color of money continues to change in America, and as it does, we learn more all the time. There are great lessons in the past. Another of the unfolding ironies is that black fine arts painters in the nineteenth century would not have been able to get works like Jones' displayed in any way that would have exposed them to large numbers of people. In terms of style and content, painters such as Henry Ossawa Tanner (1859-1937) and Edward Mitchell Bannister (1828-1901) were restricted to complying with European standards of method and subject matter.

This exhibit not only provides a brilliant snapshot, a document. It's a look through the window of America's soul. Jones stands on the shoulders of those who came before him and, like Ellington, Douglas, and Ellison, he sings the blues.

NOTES

[1] Ralph Ellison quoted in Robert G. O'Meally, (Ed.), *Living with Music: Ralph Ellison's Jazz Writings* (New York: Modern Library, 2001), 77.

[2] Ibid., 19.

[3] William S. Pollitzer, *The Gullah People and Their African Heritage* (Athens: University of Georgia Press, 1999), 106.

[4] W. E. B. DuBois, *Black Reconstruction in America: 1860-1880* (New York: Atheneum, 1992), 57.

[5] Judith Ann Carney, *Black Rice: The African Origins of Rice Cultivation in the Americas* (Cambridge: Harvard University Press, 2001), 2.

[6] Pollitzer, 27.

[7] Geoffrey Ward and Ken Burns, *Jazz: A History of America's Music* (New York: Alfred A. Knopf, 2000), 8.

[8] Grace Elizabeth Hale, *Making Whiteness: The Culture of Segregation in the South, 1890-1940* (New York: Vintage Books, 1999), 7.

Slavery
A Global Perspective

Donald West

"To accept one's past — one's history — is not the same thing as drowning in it, it is learning how to use it."

James Baldwin

Slavery has existed for millennia throughout the world and is believed to have been first practiced in Africa, the oldest and second largest continent.

Until the "New World" exploration, West Africa was the number one gold center in the world.

1300 — European Commercial Revolution created the modern system of slavery and slave trade.

1390 — African slaves brought to Europe.

1400s & 1500s — Portuguese and Spanish trading posts established along West and Central African coast.

WESTERN HEMISPHERE

Pre-colonial (1492-1526) — Black People from Europe arrived in the New World as slaves, servants, servicemen, and explorers with Europeans. One of the best known black explorers was Estevanico aka Esteban or Little Stephen who became the first non-Native American to adventure in what is now Arizona and New Mexico (1535-1539).

1492 to 1800 — Spain's American empire heavily dependent on African slave labor.

1502 — The Atlantic slave trade began in earnest.

1517 — Bishop Bartolemeo de las Casas of Spain advocated use of African slaves as surrogates for the decimated Indian laborers. The three major monotheistic religious groups of Christians, Muslims, and Jews all participated in the slave trade.

1600 to 1700 — The Netherlands monopolized the Atlantic slave trade. Later other European nations became very involved including: Britain, France, Denmark, Portugal, Prussia, Sweden, Brazil, and the United States.

1640s — Rise of West Indian sugar plantations. Profit from the slave trade and the fruits of slave labor increased the demand for African people. Between 1507 and 1870 10 million to 15 million Africans were transported as slaves to the New World, and about 5 to 8 million may have died during slave hunts and during the "Middle Passage." There are more than 27,300 documented voyages from Africa.

THE AMERICAS

Only five percent of all African slaves arrived in British North America. The greatest number of Africans enslaved were shipped to Brazil and the Caribbean.

From 1526-1865 the struggle for freedom in the Americas took on many forms including: work slow-downs, slave revolts, arson, destruction of property and equipment, use of poisons, abortions, killing of livestock, suicide, self-mutilation, infanticide, armed struggle, organized protest, litigation, escapes, and war (the Haitian Revolution, 1791 - 1803 and American Civil War, 1861 - 1865).

In response to the struggle for freedom, slave holders ruled by intimidation and terror which also took on many forms. Recalcitrant slaves would be separated or sold from families, whipped, beaten, and even branded. The dismemberment of ears, limbs or digits was employed. They were also starved to death. Public executions (including being burned at the stake to humiliate rebellious slaves as well as to discourage others) were also instituted.

The Atlantic Slave Trade yielded such high profits that Europeans came to refer to Africans as "black gold." Approximately 15 to 18 million Africans were delivered into the Islamic Trans-Saharan and Indian Ocean slave trade between 650 and 1905.

NORTH AMERICAN EXPERIENCE

1526 — The Spanish established a settlement of 500 men and women including 100 African slaves in what became known as San Miguel de Gualdape, La Florida (near present day Georgetown, South Carolina). African slaves rebelled and set fire to the colony. The slaves remained after the Spanish survivors fled back to Espanola (present day Haiti and the Dominican Republic). Thus, West Africans became the first non-Native Americans to live permanently in the present day United States.

1619 — Indentured servitude became law in Colonial Virginia. White servitude lasted for nearly 200 years.

Arrival of first Africans in British North American colony. "About the last of August...twenty Negras" (Africans) from a Dutch ship are traded in exchange for food at Jamestown and are accorded the status of "indenture servants." In the 1620s the Dutch would be the early suppliers of slaves from Africa to Virginia and to New Netherlands.

1619-1662 — Africans enjoyed the same status as English colonists. They lived in North America as servants, slaves, masters, property owners, community leaders, and even elected officials. (Mathias DeSousa was elected to Maryland's General Assembly in 1641.)

1641 — Massachusetts became the first colony to give statutory recognition to slavery. All other colonies would follow with Georgia being the last in 1750.

Since England had no laws that defined the status of a slave, the colonies made up their own. These "slave codes" protected the property rights of the master.

Late 1600s — Slave codes passed in North American colonies. Many slave codes were modeled after those in use throughout the Caribbean and South America. One of the first North American colonies to establish slave codes was South Carolina, which borrowed heavily from the content and ordinance of Barbados. These laws limited the personal movement of slaves and circumscribed every aspect of their lives.

Beginning in the 1660s, new laws gradually lowered the status of all Africans, regardless of religion. By 1747 all colonies had enacted laws to restrict the opportunities and activities of free Africans with regard to their civil liberties under British law (i.e owning weapons, voting, holding public office, serving as witnesses in court, or serving in a militia). Furthermore, in 1670 the House of Burgesses (Virginia) abridged the property rights of Africans, barring them— " though baptized and enjoying their own Freedom"— from buying the labor contracts of white servants. All other colonies soon followed.

1663 — Virginia and Maryland made all Africans and their children in the colony slaves durante vita, or for life.

1664 — Maryland enacted first antiamalgamation (miscegenation) law to prevent widespread intermarriage of white women and African men. Other colonies passed similar laws: Virginia, 1691; Massachusetts, 1705; North Carolina, 1715; South Carolina, 1717; Delaware, 1721; Pennsylvania, 1725. The miscegenation statute would be the last discriminatory policy to be removed from the legal codes of the United States of American with (Richard and Mildred) Loving v. Virginia, (1967).

1667 — Less than three years later, Maryland enacted a statute defining all blacks as slaves at birth whatever the status of their mothers.

1672 — Bounties were placed by Virginia on the heads of " Maroons," runaway slaves who formed back-country communities and sometimes raided the tidewater settlements. Maroon activity and resistance has also been well documented in Jamaica and Brazil.

1676 — The poplar uprising known as (Nathaniel) Bacon's Rebellion contributed to the emergence of a new labor system: African slavery in the Chesapeake region (Maryland and Virginia). In an effort to prevent another white rebellion and to maintain their privileged class position, the leaders of Virginia and Maryland committed themselves and their descendants to a social system based on the exploitation of African slaves. This facilitated the sharp division between black and white labor groups. Thereafter, Annapolis would become the major port city for the African slave trade in the upper South. Charleston became the major slave port city in the lower South.

1690 — Transition from white indentured to African slave labor initiated.

1738 to 1759 — The first known free black settlement in North America, Fort Gracia Real de Santa Teresa de Mose was established near St.Augustine, Florida, by escaped slaves. Escaped slaves were frequently assisted by Native Americans including Creek, Yemassee, Yuchi, and Seminole.

News of Fort Mose reached as far north as the Carolinas, and its location was regarded as a contributing factor to the worst slave insurrection of the 1700s.

September 9, 1739 — A series of slave revolts swept the countryside near Charleston, South Carolina resulting in the deaths of 51 whites and many more slaves. The major slave rebellion known as Stono was led by a man named Jemmy. At least 20 to 25 white people were killed before the insurrection was put down. South Carolina briefly considered ending slavery; instead they enacted the toughest slave codes or restrictions in the colonies. These included restricting the number of African imports, diversifying the ethnicity of the African slave labor population, and taking drums away in an effort to prevent slaves from using the instruments as a way of communicating with one another.

For nearly 85 years after Fort Mose ended operations, Florida continued to be a refuge for many escaped slaves from the southeast, and a persistent source of conflict between slave owners and Africans seeking to preserve their freedom.

1772 — Responding to a petition inspired by Granville Sharp, Lord Chief Justice Mansfield abolished slavery in the United Kingdom, stating: "Is not a Negro a Man?"...As soon as any slave sets foot on English soil he shall be free." The British ended slavery in all of its colonies by 1834.

July 4, 1776 — The revolutionary principles of liberty and equality which had clear implications for enslaved Africans was omitted. In an earlier draft of the Declaration of Independence, Thomas Jefferson had indicted the king of England for having violated the "most sacred rights of life and liberty of a distant people, who never offended him, captivating them into slavery in another hemisphere...." Eighty-six changes were made. The section denouncing slavery was deleted "in complaisance to South Carolina and Georgia."

July 30, 1776 — In a discussion and debate with other members of the Continental Congress, Benjamin Franklin, a well-know foe of slavery, made his case for termination of human bondage during the Revolutionary War Period. In his remarks about the value and importance of slavery, he warned his fellow countrymen that " slaves rather weaken than strengthen the State, and there is therefore some difference between them and sheep; sheep will never make any insurrections." Again in 1790, Franklin asked the first Congress of the United States to do what the Continental Congress had not done: abolish slavery.

1783 — Elizabeth Freeman, born in Africa (around 1742) and sold as a slave won her freedom by claiming in a Massachusetts court that the "inherent liberty" of all applied to slaves as well. As a consequence of Freeman's demand, as well as the petition for freedom on the basis of Revolutionary principles made by other slaves, the state Supreme Court abolished slavery in Massachusetts.

1787 — The US Constitution adopted with pro-slavery provisions and the establishment of white preferential treatment.

1791 — Haitian Revolution led by Toussaint L'Ouverture (who referred to himself as the "Black Napoleon") began with a revolt of 100,000 slaves in the northwestern province. France with the help of Denmark, Spain, and even long time adversary, the United Kingdom, could not recapture the island nation. Between 1800-1803, Napoleon Bonaparte, the emperor of France, lost nearly 25,000 troops in an unsuccessful attempt to retake Haiti. There were nearly 60,000 casualties between 1791 and 1803, which included the allied forces of the other nations. Haiti became the second independent nation in the western hemisphere in 1804.

Napoleon, fatigued from the unsuccessful military campaign against Haiti, decided to give up his plans for reestablishing or building an empire in North America. In 1803 he sold the Louisiana Territory to the United States for about 15 million dollars. This acquisition doubled the size of the United States.

February 12, 1793 — the first fugitive slave law enacted by Congress. The bill made it a criminal offense to harbor a fugitive slave or prevent his arrest.

1793 — Eli Whitney received credit for inventing the cotton engine. It is widely accepted among historians that Whitney got the idea and design from slaves who, in fact, had been using such a device for several years in the Savannah, Georgia area before he arrived there as a teacher. Up until this point, most whites, including many slave owners, believed slavery was dying out. This invention would ultimately contribute more to the growth and expansion of slavery, bringing new vitality to slavery as cotton would replace tobacco as the number one cash crop in the United States.

The improved cotton gin spurred plantation production. With the cotton gin, one person could clean 50 times more cotton in a day than by hand. Within one year, Southern cotton production increased twelve-fold. In eight years, it increased more than 250 times. By the 1830s, the U.S. was the number one cotton exporter in the world. From 1790 onward slavery became essentially an exclusively southern institution.

The Northeast was well on its way to ending slavery at the time of Whitney's invention. Vermont, not yet admitted to statehood, passed a law ending slavery in 1777 during the American Revolution. New York implemented a gradual emancipation program in 1799 thus abolishing slavery officially in 1827. By 1804, all of the states north of Delaware had taken steps to abolish slavery gradually. New Jersey was the last state, in 1804. As late as 1860, however, there were still some slaves in New Jersey.

Slavery died in the North because it was not economically feasible and as a direct result of forces set in motion by the "Rights of Man" movement, a popular Revolutionary War theme.

January 30, 1797 — Congress rejected first recorded petition from African Americans on ending slavery. The plea, from escaped slaves, asked Congress to consider "our relief as a people."

1799 — Seventy-four members of the Free African Society petitioned Congress to end the slave trade and for the protection of black people against kidnapping by slave catchers. The petition also asked that Africans "be allowed to partake of the liberties" to which they were entitled. The request, which had been sent "to the President, Senate and House of Representatives," was rejected by the House after a brief debate 85 to 1.

1807 — The United Kingdom ended the Atlantic slave trade. A world-wide effort ending the slave trade followed, thereafter. The United States ended the trade in 1808. However, U.S. enforcement of the law was so weak that about 100,000 more abducted Africans entered the country illegally before slavery ended.

1809 — Tecumseh's message of Pan-Indian unity included a warning that Indians faced possible loss of land, culture, and eventually enslavement like African Americans if they did not resist white expansion.

1820s — Internal (Domestic) slave trade boom started. Shortly after Congress banned the Atlantic slave trade in 1808, the practice of breeding African slaves for the purpose of selling them to the highest bidder was conducted by all slave states, with Virginia, Maryland, and Louisiana the three leading states. By 1860, nearly 4 million African Americans were slaves.

March 3, 1820 — Missouri Compromise enacted prohibiting slavery North of 36 degrees 30 parallel or the Southwestern corner of the newly admitted state (Missouri). Despite the concession to reduce the spread of slavery by both the North and South, the issue of human bondage would thereafter become the center of social and political issues. At the same time the slave issue was growing in this country, other Western nations had begun to abolish slavery (Mexico, 1829).

1820 to 1865 — Dozens of anti-slavery societies in the North and South agitated for the end of slavery. Southern organizational activities declined after the Nat Turner Rebellion. From August 21-23, 1831, Nat Turner, a slave and lay minister led the most successful slave revolt in American history. Sixty white people and countless numbers of slaves were killed, some on only the strength of rumors of their involvement. Turner was eventually captured and was executed on November 11 in Jerusalem, Virginia.

August 1, 1834 — Slavery was abolished throughout the British Empire, including Southern Africa and the Caribbean.

July, 1839 — A slave rebellion, led by Sengebe Pieh (Joseph Cinquez) aboard La Amistad became the most celebrated slave mutiny in the history of the transatlantic slave trade. Between 1699 and 1845 there were 150 documented cases of rebellions aboard slave ships. Only one was successful in returning Africans to their place of origin. This was the Amistad Mutiny led by Cinquez. In a case involving the United States and Spain, the U.S. Supreme Court ruled in favor of the Africans. In 1841 the 35 survivors were set free and returned to Africa the following year. Another slave mutiny involved the Creole, a vessel en route from Virginia to New Orleans, which was granted asylum and freedom in the Bahamas (1841).

The Compromise of 1850 which included a stronger fugitive slave law precipitated black migration from the United States. Some estimates suggest that as many as 1,200 refugees settled in Canada every year from 1850 to 1860. Thousands were aided by people like William Lloyd Garrison, Robert Purvis, William Still, Lewis Tappan, Levi Coffin, John Mason, and Harriet Tubman.

1852 — Harriet Beecher Stowe, published *Uncle Tom's Cabin*, a novel that deeply stirred the hearts of the people of the North against the enslavement of black people in America. In less than 12 months, Stowe's novel sold more than 300,000. The tragic story of a slave aroused popular sentiment toward a single cause: the issue of slavery. In 1863, when President Abraham Lincoln first met Mrs. Stowe, he remarked, " so you're the little woman who wrote the book that made this great war." In many regards, this book had the same impact, popularizing anti-slavery feelings, as did Thomas Paine's pamphlet *Common Sense* on the issue of Independence during the American Revolution period.

More than one hundred and thirty-five years later another novel would help to revisit the issue of slavery and the extent slaves might go to gain freedom for themselves and their children. Toni Morrison's novel *Beloved*, which won the 1988 Pulitzer Prize for fiction is based on the tragic story of Margaret Garner. In 1856, Garner and seven other slaves, including her three children escaped from Kentucky across the Ohio River to freedom in Cincinnati. Her owner Archibald Grimes, who is believed to have fathered at least two of Margaret's children, pursued them. With a court order and a U.S. Marshal they were captured, though not before Garner slit the throat of her daughter with a butcher knife rather than see the child returned to slavery. She was disarmed before she could kill her two sons. Morrison's novel was made into a major motion picture by Oprah Winfrey in 1998.

March 6, 1857 — Dred Scott v. Sanford. In a sweeping decision, the U.S. Supreme Court, pronounced that blacks could not be considered citizens of the United States. The Court also declared that blacks had no rights that a white man was required to respect. The case further weakened efforts by some in government to prevent the expansion of slavery.

1859 — John Brown and 17 other men including, including five blacks, attacked a federal arsenal at Harpers Ferry, Virginia. Two of the blacks accompanying Brown were killed in the shoot-out and two were later hanged (December 16). Brown and two other white men were also hanged. They were found guilty of treason and creating an insurrection. Speaking of his courage and conviction, twenty-two years later in an address delivered at a Harpers Ferry College, Frederick Douglass said " John Brown began the war that ended slavery and made this a free republic. Until this blow was struck, the prospect for freedom was dim, shadowy, and uncertain."

1860 — The black population of the U.S. was 4,401,830, about 14 per cent of the total; almost a half million blacks were non-slaves, and of these slightly more than half lived in the southern states.

1861 — Confederates attacked Fort Sumter in Charleston, South Carolina, starting the Civil War; on hearing the news, Frederick Douglass, the most recognized black Abolitionist, cried out: "God be praised!" Free blacks responded in large numbers to Lincoln's initial call for 75,000 volunteers but were turned down. Eventually nearly 200,000 African Americans served in the army and navy to preserve the union and end slavery.

1862 — President Abraham Lincoln issued preliminary Emancipation Proclamation (September 22).

1863 — When Douglass was recruiting black men for the Union army during the Civil War, he urged them to " remember Denmark Vesey." He was referring to the leader of an attempted slave insurrection during the Summer of 1822. The plot, referred to by John Hope Franklin as "the most elaborate... conspiracy of the period," involving as many as 9,000 free and enslaved Africans, was foiled in Charleston, South Carolina. One hundred and thirty arrests were made, and 35 men, including Vesey, were executed. Four white men said to be involved were fined and incarcerated, as well.

1865 — The 13th Amendment was ratified December 18, ending slavery (Mississippi ratified the Amendment March 20, 1995). The United States became only the second nation in the Western Hemisphere in which slavery was ended as a result of war. Haiti was the first.

Puerto Rico and Cuba, Spanish colonies, ended slavery in 1873 and 1880, respectively. Decades after first promising, Brazil ended slavery in 1888. The League of Nations and its successor the United Nations continued worldwide efforts to end slavery.

1945 — Declaration of Human Rights specifically prohibited slavery as well as the slave trade and condemned forced labor.

The Western Hemisphere experienced three different slave systems. The first, practiced by the Dutch, Danish, British and American colonies, had no effective tradition, no slave rights, and little religious influence. The second, which was typically found among Indians as well as Africans, had slave law and a belief in the sanctity of the person, The French combined elements of both to create a third form. The Spanish and Portuguese encouraged church attendance and incorporated many provisions favoring manumission. Though the institution of slavery varied, however, it represented abject and inhuman cruelty. Nevertheless, the indomitable character of the human spirit resulted in the retention of Africanism in the Americas which includes religion, music, art, storytelling, language, architecture, agriculture, and culinary traditions. Efforts to improve race relations need to start with these origins of black history and culture, and the issue of slavery must be addressed as an important primary step to reconciliation.

RESOURCES

From Slavery to Freedom: A History of Negro Americans, 8th Edition, John Hope Franklin & Alfred A. Moss, Jr.

A Shining Thread of Hope: The History of Black Women in America, Darlene Clark Hine & Kathleen Thompson.

A Turbulent Voyage: Readings in African American Studies, Floyd W. Hayes, III.

The Destruction of Black Civilization: Great Issues of a Race from 4500 B.C. to 2000 A.D., Chancellor Williams.

The Problem of Slavery in Western Culture, David B. Davis.

Family Across the Sea: Viewer's Guide and Video, SCETV.

Black Cargoes: A History of the Atlantic Slave Trade, Daniel P. Mannix in collaboration with Malcolm Cowley.

Capitalism and Slavery, Eric Williams.

The African Slave Trade, Basil Davidson.

Caribbean, Sugar and Slaves, Richard Dunn.

The Interesting Narrative of the Life of Olaudah Equiano, written by Himself, [Ed.] Robert J. Allison.

"The Hidden History of Slave Trading in Antebellum South Carolina: John Spring III and Other 'Gentlemen Dealing in Slaves'," Michael Tadman. *South Carolina Historical Magazine* January 1996, Vol 97, No1.

African Americans in the Colonial Era: From African Origins through the American Revolution, Donald Wright

The Wolf by the Ears: Thomas Jefferson and Slavery, John Chester Miller.

The Slave Community, John Blassingame.

The Gullah: Rice, Slavery, and the Sierra Leone-American Connection, Joseph A Opala.

Black Leaders of the Nineteenth Century, [Ed.] Leon Litwack & August Meier.

The Color of Money
Background and Commentary

Richard G. Doty

You may be wondering why all those slaves appeared on Southern bank notes. As far as that goes, what were banks doing issuing their own currency? They can't do so now; how could they get away with it then?

Banks issued their own paper money because of the country's past history. For the first two centuries of our story, we lacked precious metals, the essential elements for making coinage. People came up with a paper alternative as early as 1690 in Massachusetts and 1703 in South Carolina, the second colony to issue currency. By the middle of the eighteenth century all of the original colonies had issued paper at one time or another.

These currencies were *official.* They were printed on behalf of colonial governments, circulated by them, and guaranteed by them. Authorities in London viewed these goings-on with a critical eye, and they made occasional half-hearted attempts to either rein them in or ban them altogether. But the issues continued, with or without the blessing of the Crown: paper money was simply too useful and too important to give up.

When the colonies revolted against England, they expected to finance the War for Independence in the same fashion as they had paid for earlier campaigns on Britain's behalf: they expected to pay the bills with paper money, redeemable in coin after an American victory. But three elements would have to be in place for the scheme to work as it had before. The war would have to be short. It would have to be local and contained. And the British would have to send coinage to retire the paper money at war's end, just as they had been doing ever since the 1690s.

What the insurgents actually got was the precise opposite of what they needed, or expected. They got a war which went on and on, year after year, with no victory in sight until the very end. They got a war which involved actual or potential occupation of most of the country at one time or another. And what they did *not* get was a triumphant peace, after which a remorseful England would send coinage to redeem their paper.

They did get something else: they experienced the worst monetary depreciation this country has ever seen. If we assume that a one-dollar federal note, called Continental Currency, could be freely exchanged for a "Mexican dollar" (the famous Piece of Eight) in 1776, by the end of the decade, it would have taken forty dollars in Continental Currency (or more than fifty, if you had South Carolina money) to get that same silver Piece of Eight– if you could find anybody foolish enough to part with it at any price!

Victory at Yorktown came just in time: the battered insurgent monetary system was given time to revive. But members of the business community looked back at the experience and collectively shuddered. If they had their way, their new country would be one where coinage was king.

They put their sentiments and aspirations into a new document called the Constitution. Composed in 1787, made law by 1789, the Constitution spelled out precisely who could issue money, who could not, and what form that money would assume:

Only the national government could issue coinage.

No state could issue coinage, which some had been doing since the mid-1780s.

No state could issue "bills of credit."

With a look back at the debacle with Continental Currency, the Constitution was mum on whether or not the national government could issue paper money. The men who wrote the new law would very much rather that it did not; but they were also realists, and they knew that it might someday have to do so. So they neither prohibited nor espoused federal currency. Instead, they swept the issue under the rug and hoped for the best.

That best would be a plentiful national coinage, from an efficient national mint. But the best did not happen, could not happen: we had no more precious metal now than we had had in the days of the colonies, and while a United States Mint was indeed set up in 1792, it would be a minor player for the next forty years. Even had raw materials been available, the Mint would not have been able to turn them into coins quickly enough to keep up with the growing population and the burgeoning economy. Some other medium of exchange was needed, and needed quickly. If states were out of the money business altogether, and the federal government unable or unwilling to meet the challenge, what was left?

Banks were left. The Constitution was silent on whether banks could circulate paper money (probably because Alexander Hamilton and his colleagues had not foreseen an occasion in which they might need to do so). A few private, note-issuing banks had been set up in the 1780s, pumping their products into the nation's anemic fiscal bloodstream. A few more came into existence in the 1790s, and many more after 1800. South Carolina alone had twenty– most of them centered in Charleston, but several also doing business in places ranging from Camden to Winnsboro.

To keep up with the nation's potential, an almost unlimited amount of currency would be required. In turn, this meant that the country's printing technology needed to be greatly improved. Fortunately, the right person appeared at the right time-- Jacob Perkins, of Newburyport, Massachusetts. Perkins was an inventor, self-promoter, and jack of all trades. He was also a genius. He invented a way of engraving on steel rather than copper, which expanded the life of a printing plate by a factor of six. Of even greater significance, he came up with a way of mass-producing engraved images, then carrying them from a master to a working steel plate. Perkins created the potential for the *industrialization of money*– the creation of an infinite number of notes, all of them identical. Since absolute identity between one note and another was and is absolutely essential for the prevention and detection of counterfeits, Perkins had solved several problems at the same time. His was the key that unlocked the potential of the American private bank note.

But his genius was carried in other directions by the bankers he sought to serve. He assumed that bankers everywhere would want identical notes, which his technology could supply in short order. He misjudged his audience: what the bankers wanted was *variety*– fancy scenes, portraits, and beautiful designs which would tell the public about the bankers and their institutions, which would tempt the public to accept their notes in preference to others. If Perkins were unable or unwilling to give the bankers what they wanted, they would find other printers for the purpose; and the latter would do the job, *using Perkins' technology for the purpose.*

That was what happened, and that was how people of color came to America's currency– along with Native Americans, women, farmers, railroad trains, steamboats, George Washington, John C. Calhoun and anything or anybody else you can imagine– or which could be imagined a century and a half ago.

But this doesn't explain *why* people of color came to America's currency. When we consider that question, things become interesting indeed.

Whatever its nature, money reflects something of the world in which it is created, of which it forms a part. This has always been the case, although the connections have often been subtle and difficult to appreciate. But sometimes the opposite holds true: in a time of war, money is likely to change dramatically, reflecting rapid alterations and tensions in the larger world, even anticipating them. The decade or so between the Compromise of 1850 and the outbreak of the 1861 war provides us with one of the clearest links between our money and outside events. People of color were at its center.

There had been sectional tensions in the United States well prior to mid-century. Slavery was a central element, but so were political competition, differing economies and different ways of looking at the world. They were inevitable results of a huge country and a fairly small, widely scattered population. But the Mexican War provided a flash point. The Americans had done rather well in that conflict, becoming the proud possessors of lands all the way to the Pacific Coast. Now increased sectionalism raised its head: which section would control the new lands, and whose labor system would prevail there? Each side felt threatened by the other and while a political deal was cobbled together in 1850, it satisfied no one. Sectional tensions would prevail through the next decade, growing deeper through time. Slaves, and the system which they supported and in turn produced them, stood at the center of everything. So it was only natural that they would begin appearing on our money.

They already had, once before. Around 1820 (at a time when the members of an earlier generation had been at loggerheads over sectional competition and slavery), the Farmers & Mechanics Bank of Augusta, Georgia had ordered notes in four denominations but with a single vignette. The vignette was a representation of black and white workers, slave and free. Slaves were working in a cotton field in one part of the vignette; a flatboat loaded with their produce was being poled along a river in another. The scene was matter-of-fact, non-judgmental; virtually nothing like it would be seen again for the next thirty years.

Then came the tensions of the 1850s. Slavery and the African American were on every-body's mind. Southern bankers were no exception, and some of them now thought of putting slave scenes on their currency. Northern printers (security printing was a virtual Northern monopoly, most of the work being done in New York, Boston, and Philadelphia) were caught off-guard when bankers in South Carolina, Georgia, or Alabama asked them for notes with slave vignettes. There previously never having been such requests, the printers had no ready-made images in stock, and the creation of new ones from scratch took time and cost money. What to do? The printers *reworked their extant images, changing white to black, and free labor to slave labor.*

You can see the results in this display. The central vignette on a dollar bill from the Adrian Insurance Company, of Adrian, Michigan was retouched for a five-dollar bill from Winnsboro, South Carolina; and a group of whites harvesting grain became a group of slaves picking cotton. By the same process, a white farmhand on a note from Washington, DC had his clothing tattered and his skin darkened– and emerged as a slave on a bill from Howardsville, Virginia. The process was repeated elsewhere over the next few years, and it bought breathing space for the Northern printers and the Southern bankers whom they served.

In passing, it might be observed that, if security printers now had to have *two* sets of images, one of each race, one for each section, the threat of disunity was becoming rather more than a threat.

Printers got the time they needed to create completely new images, and they found a ready sale to bankers from Louisiana to Virginia. This second phase of slave representation occupied the middle years of the 1850s, and it was distinguished by an unadorned realism. Slaves tended to appear in agri-cultural scenes (which was accurate in and of itself: that was why they had been brought to America in the first place). They picked, baled, and moved cotton from field to market. They cut sugar cane and transported that commodity. They were almost always found in the field rather than the factory, because the slave in the mill was a concept which frightened whites in both sections, if for different reasons. (For the Northern white, he represented a threat, and for his Southern counterpart a difficulty: if he had the intelligence to operate a machine, why was he a slave?) While vignettes of this second type continued to enjoy popularity, they were partially eclipsed by a third set of images, the most interesting of all because of their intimate connection with larger events.

In the larger scheme of things, the debate over slavery, and the drift of the sections away from each other, intensified rather than diminished as time went on. The year 1852 saw the publication of *Uncle Tom's Cabin*, whose scathing denunciation of slavery and sympathetic description of slaves had an effect roughly equivalent to an earthquake on opinion in both North and South. The year 1853 saw the Gadsden Purchase– seen as the basis for a southern-route transcontinental railroad by some, as leading to the spread of an odious institution, by others. The year 1854 saw the beginnings of the troubles over Kansas, where Northern and Southern farm boys would gain practice in marksmanship which would come in handy in the times to come. And so it went, year after year, through the remainder of the decade. The North looked with increasing revulsion on the South and its " peculiar institution." The South told the North to mind its own business and leapt to slavery's defense. It would portray that institution as a positive good and broadcast the news to anyone within reach. One of the ways in which it would do so was through its money.

Southern bank notes featuring vignettes sympathetic to slavery would be good for Southern morale. But they might do some good up North as well: private bank notes circulated nationally, even if they were created locally. The experiment would be tried.

The new depictions would continue to center on agriculture. But the appearance of the slaves would change. One smiled at the onlooker on a fifty-dollar bill from Montgomery, Alabama: surely, he was enjoying his work, and that work must be beneficial to America, and to him! An amiable chucklehead, he dreamed and dozed his life away; it was just as well that he was in bondage, so feeble was his mentality.

In other words, this was a person with great, natural limitations, in slavery for his own good. His limitations might be suggested by his placement vis-à-vis whites. The central vignette on a Hamburg, South Carolina five-dollar bill took a typical approach: we see a slave and his master, and there can be no question of who had the superior role, who the inferior one.

But there was one view, which overshadowed all the others. It was engraved in 1857. It struck a very responsive chord, did so very quickly, and was used by banks across the South for the next several years. It depicted a slave mother and child. She smiled, and her infant laughed aloud while clutching a tiny bough of the produce which kept them both in bondage.

Images of slaves continiued in use after the outbreak of war in 1861. Several issues of the Confederacy featured bondsmen– including a hundred-dollar bill of 1861 which pirated a Northern cut originally done for a Mississippi bank in 1838! The most popular Confederate vignette showed slaves hoeing cotton, and it too was adapted from a Northern engraving (for a two-dollar bill from the Bank of Savannah, which went into circulation just as the war was beginning). But it was translated from engraving to lithography, a reflection of the insurgent section's technological limitations.

The wartime South added some images to the portfolio. Most of them returned to the realistic approach, wherein slaves worked in the fields or hauled the products of the fields to market. In several instances, they appeared on money from the *states* rather than that of banks, a reflection of the states' right mentality which guided the insurgents: the creation of money could be an attribute of sovereignty, and the states were sovereign once more. Other wartime images were created for banks and related institutions, and their quality and artistry ranged from a sophisticated lithograph (on a five-dollar bill of the Georgia Savings Bank, created by the firm responsible for Confederate currency) to a crude woodcut (on a three-dollar bill from Brenham, Texas, created by a nameless up-country job printer).

Images of African Americans outlasted the war by a few years. The pieces of paper on which they appeared were not, technically, currency, but in a cash-strapped South they served as money all the same. A number of them recycled images originally created for Southern banks prior to 1861: a drowsing man on a cart hauling cotton started out on a note from Macon, Georgia, ended up on a bond from the state of South Carolina. Others were apparently created for the occasion, such as the central vignette on a scrip issue of the Macon & Brunswick Railroad Company. But prewar and postwar images are all very much alike when not identical. And from that, we might conclude that the status of the African American had not changed all that much, regardless of the war which had just been fought, and that custom would prove stronger than legal intention for a long time to come.

NOTES

Richard G. Doty, *America's Money - America's Story: A Comprehensive Chronicle of American Numismatic History*. (Iola, WI: Krause Publications, 1998).

Richard G. Doty, [Ed.] *America's Currency, 1789-1866*. Proceedings of the Second Coinage of the Americas Conference, New York, 1985. (New York: American Numismatic Society, 1986).

Richard G. Doty, *Pictures from a Distant Country*. (In preparation).

Richard G. Doty, " Surviving images, forgotten peoples: Native Americans, women, and African Americans on United States obsolete banknotes." in *The Banker's Art: Studies in Paper Money*, pp. 118-131, ed. Virginia Hewitt (London: British Museum Press, 1995).

James A. Haxby, *Standard Catalog of United States Obsolete Bank Notes, 1782-1866*, 4 vols. (Iola, WI: Krause Publications, 1988).

Guy R. Swanson, "Agents of culture and nationalism: the Confederate Treasury and Confederate currency," in *The Banker's Art: Studies in Paper Money*, pp. 132-139, ed. Virginia Hewitt (London: British Museum Press, 1995).

The Images

First Image

During the Colonial era, blacks and whites were categorized as indentured servants, until early laws were enacted forcing black indentured servants into slave labor. The idea of black subordination evolved over time and was still being established in 1820 when the first image of blacks on United States currency appeared.

"First Image" is the first know depiction of African Americans on American money. Unlike the images which follow it, there is no apparent suggestion of subordination in the relationships between blacks and whites in the scene. Note how artist John W. Jones conveys this point visually by comparing his rendering of the sky in "First Image" to that in "Overseer with Whip."

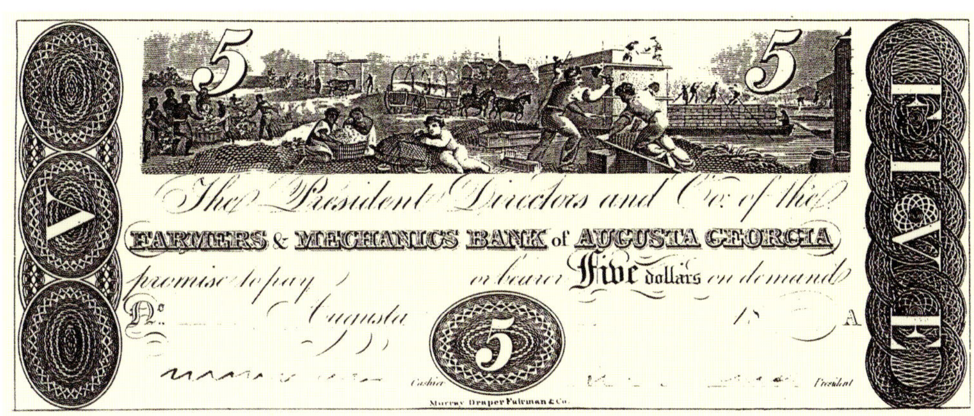

1 First Image

Collection of Dr. Al Fraser

CITIZENS BANK
THREE DOLLARS
STATE OF
VIRGINIA
CITIZENS BANK
THREE DOLLARS
STATE OF
VIRGINIA

Recycled Images

After independence, support for centralized government in the United States was encouraged among rebellious and disenfranchised white laborers through creation of permanently subordinate black slave caste available for economic exploitation. The demand for images of slavery on Southern currency, which came about as part of the growing importance of the "slavery question," caught printers off guard. They responded by changing their existing images of white people into black slaves

The engraving of a white farmer carrying a basket of corn used by the Citizens Bank of Washington, DC becomes a black slave carrying the same basket of corn on a note issued by the Bank of Howardsville, Virginia.

2 Slave Picking Corn

Collection of Dr. Harold Rhodes III

The engraving of a solitary rider stopped to watch a group of white harvesters used by the Adrian Insurance Company of Michigan becomes an overseer of black slaves on a note issued by the Planters Bank of Fairfield, South Carolina.

3 Slave Overseer With Whip

Collection of Dr. Harold Rhodes III

The engraving of a wagon team used by the Central Bank of Virginia becomes a wagon team of Whites on horseback and black slaves on a note issued by the Planters Bank of Fairfield, South Carolina.

4 Slave Wagon Team

Collection of Dr. Harold Rhodes III

5 Admiring Their Slaves

Collection of Dr. Alan Rashford

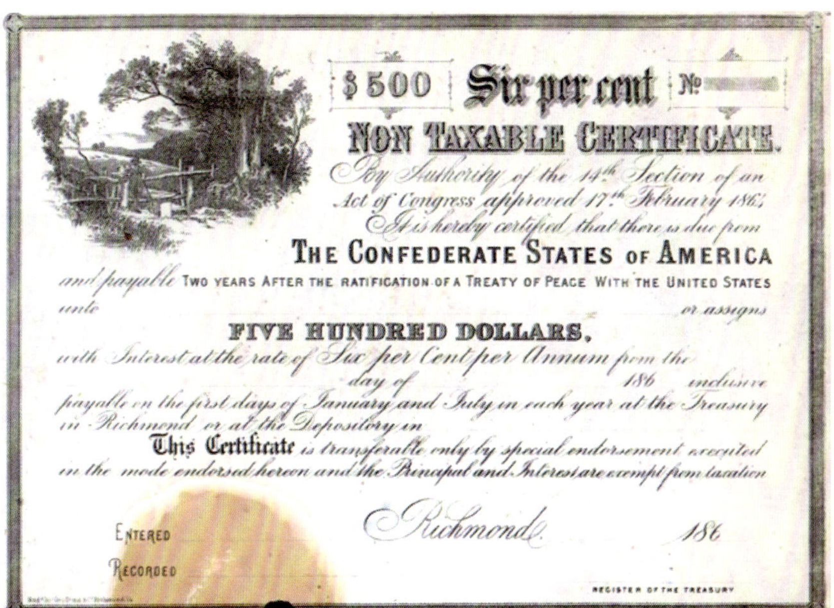

$500 Six per cent №

NON TAXABLE CERTIFICATE.

By Authority of the 14th Section of an Act of Congress approved 17th February 186,

It is hereby certified that there is due from

THE CONFEDERATE STATES OF AMERICA

and payable TWO YEARS AFTER THE RATIFICATION OF A TREATY OF PEACE WITH THE UNITED STATES unto or assigns

FIVE HUNDRED DOLLARS,

with Interest at the rate of Six per Cent per Annum from the day of 186 inclusive payable on the first days of January and July in each year at the Treasury in Richmond or at the Depository in

This Certificate is transferable only by special endorsement executed in the mode endorsed hereon and the Principal and Interest are exempt from taxation

Richmond 186

ENTERED

RECORDED

REGISTER OF THE TREASURY

6 Slave Taking A Rest

Collection of Les Payne

7 Slave Butchering Hog

Collection of John W. Jones

8 Slave Farmer

Collection of Stanley Sneed

9 Slave Tilling Ground

Collection of Dr. Harold Rhodes III

10 The Grinder and Slave

Collection of Dr. Harold Rhodes III

11 Female Slave

Collection of Donald K. Murphy

12 Slave at Mill Door

Collection of Dr. Harold Rhodes III

No 2403
THIS CERTIFIES THAT THERE HAS BEEN DEPOSITED IN THE
GEORGIA SAVINGS BANK
Five Dollars
FIVE
MACON, Ga
Cash!
Pres.

Roman Goddess of Money

Within the slaveocracy, exploitation was economic, political, socio-cultural, even biological and physical in character. New groups of people such as mulattos emerged and were enslaved, thereby expanding the numbers of the slave caste. In the image titled "Slave Profits," engravers recycled a classic mythical figure to legitimate slavery. Moneta, a Roman goddess of money, claims the riches of an enslaved labor system seen toiling in the background; they work, and she gets the money. In recycling the myth once more, notice how the artist John W. Jones chooses to tell the story. Compare his creation of the goddess with that of the engraver in his rendering of Moneta.

GEORGIA SAVINGS BANK
THIS CERTIFIES THAT THERE HAS BEEN DEPOSITED IN THE
Five Dollars
FIVE
MACON, Ga.
Cash.
Pres.

13 Slave Profits

Collection of Dr. Harold Rhodes III

CENTRAL BANK
OF TENNESSEE
Will pay ONE DOLLAR to the bearer
on demand.
NASHVILLE,
ONE

Custom Engraving

Agitation against slavery assumed a critical importance by the end of the 1850s. Banks and engravers were very deliberate in portraying the importance of African American slave labor to the economic development of the South and the nation. Scenes of agricultural labor, dominated, including cotton, tobacco, sugar cane and turpentine. Images also reveal how slavery influenced every aspect of daily life in the United States, including the introduction of such dietary staples as sugar, rice, and poultry, as well as such luxury items as tobacco.

Banks and engravers told a story of slavery that glorified, justified, and ratified an inhumane institution. John W. Jones on the other hand, tells a story of strong and indomitable character, the will to survive and carry on the qualities brought from Africa. Look at how the artist uses light and color to tell this story. Notice how the clothing of these noble people is depicted in the colors of precious gems.

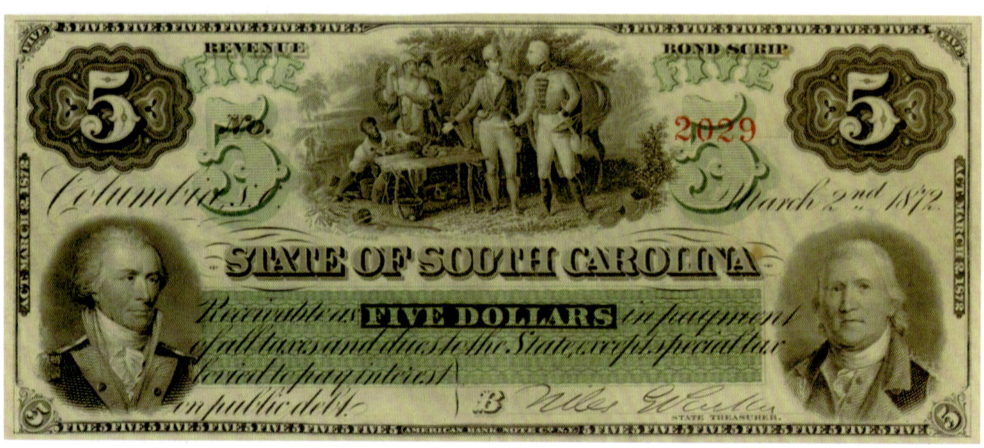

14 Slave Cooking Dinner

Collection of Dr. Harold Rhodes III

15 Slaves Working at Plantation

Collection of Rev. Jesse Hawkins

16 Slaves Loading Sugarcane

Collection of Dr. Alan Rashford

17 Slaves at Sugarcane Planation

Collection of Dr. Betty Lovelace

18 Slave Horsing Hay

Collection of Dr. Harold Rhodes III

19 Slave Carrying Wheat

Collection of Bishop A. L. Campbell

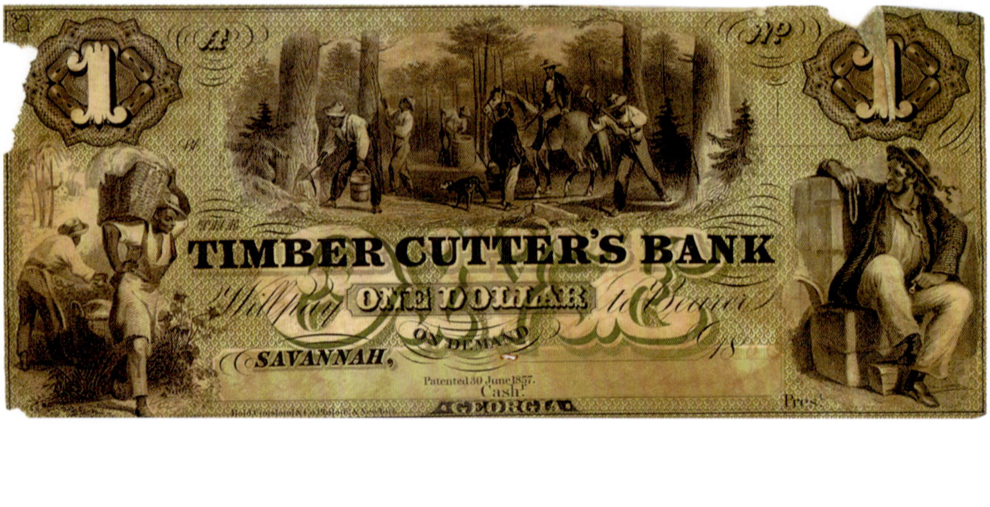

20 Slaves Harvesting Turpentine

Collection of Dr. Harold Rhodes III

21 Texas Slave

Collection of Dr. Alan Rashford

22 Slave Saddling Horse

Private Collection

23 The Slave Deal

Collection of Ann Pryde

FARMERS & EXCHANGE BANK
OF CHARLESTON
Ten Dollars
Charleston, S.C.
Cash.r

Cotton is King

New industries emerged from the slave trade and the slaves' production, including shipping and transportation, chemicals and textiles, banking, insurance and newspaper publishing.

Within agriculture, the cotton crop was king. By the 1830s the United States was the number one cotton exporter in the world. Currency from the deep South tells an extensive story of enslaved Africans and the crop that bonded them, from planting to picking to loading to shipping.

The image titled "Slave Carrying Cotton" was used on 21 different currencies. Notice how the features of the Slave Carrying Cotton, although female, emphasize the strength necessary to do the work of a man. Men, women and children were all valued property of profit.

24 Slave Carrying Cotton

Collection of Dr. Harold Rhodes III

25 Slaves Lifting Cotton Bales

Collection of Benjamin & Joyce White

26 Mississippi Slave

Collection of Nathalie Dupree

27 Slaves Clearing Field

Collection of Polly Sheppard

28 Slave Sowing Seeds

Collection of Dr. Al Fraser

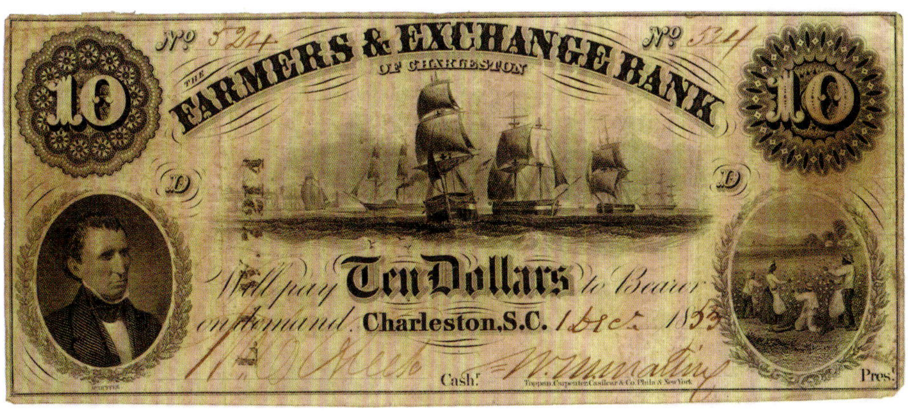

29 Slave Family Picking Cotton

Collection of Dr. Jack Bass

30 Slaves Hoeing Cotton

Collection of Ronald O. and Mittie R. Smith

31 Slave Cotton Pickers

Collection of Rev. Dr. Wayne D. Pokorny

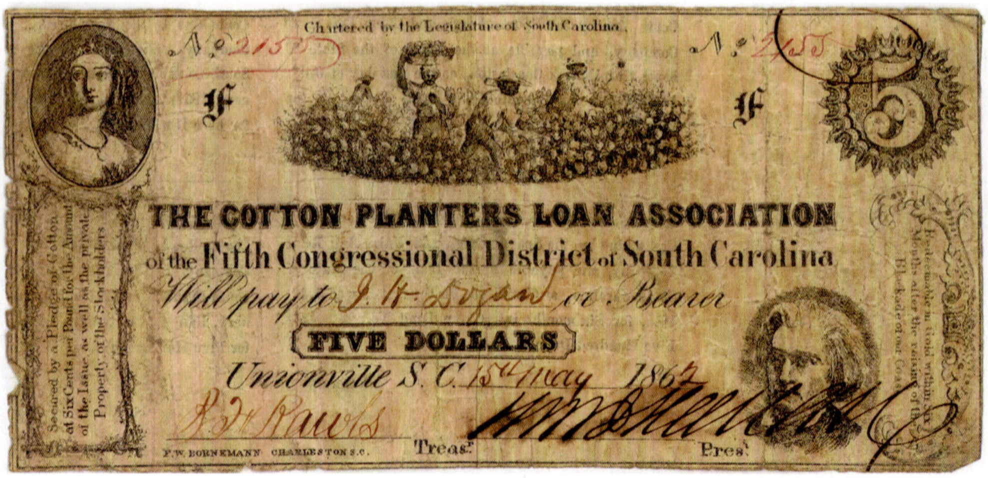

32 Slaves in Cotton Field

Collection of Dr. Harold Rhodes III

33 Slave Harvesting Cotton

Collection of Sybil Y. Parson

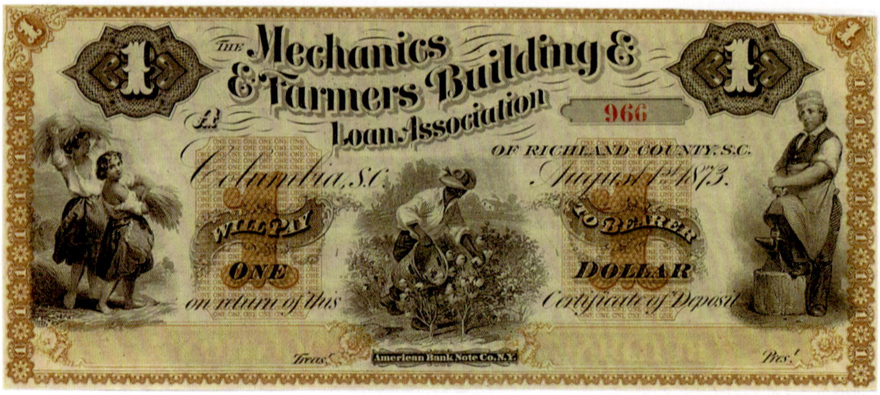

34 Slave Gathering Cotton

Collection of Juanita Legree

35 Slaves Tending Cotton

Collection of David and Alfreda Belton

36 Slaves at Work

Collection of Curtis and Dr. Vivian C. Dillihunt

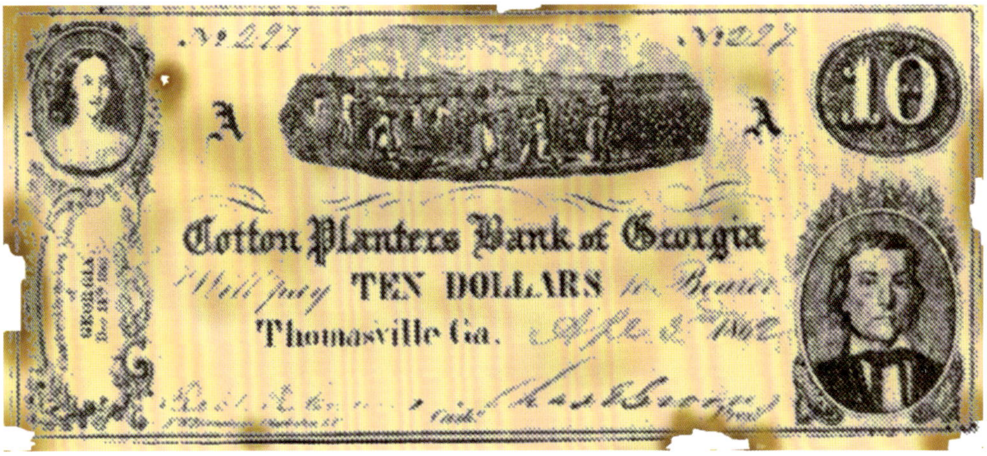

37 Field Slaves

Collection of Lane Schofield

38 Slaves Bagging Cotton

Collection of Nat Simmons

39 Slave Overseer With Whip II

Collection of Pearl Ascue

40 Slaves Harvesting Wheat

Private Collection

41 Slaves Waiting on the Train

Collection of Rodger Womack

42 Slaves Hauling Cotton

Collection of Dr. Harold Rhodes III

43 Slaves Loading Cotton

Collection of Dr. Harold Rhodes III

44 Slaves Loading Wagon

Collection of Bishop A. L. Campbell

45 Slave Herding Cotton Bales

Collection of John and Dorothy Walton

46 Slave Leading Cattle

Collection of Dr. Harold Rhodes III

47 Slave Conveying Cotton Bales

Collection of Ann Pryde

48 Slave Transporting Cotton

Collection of Benjamin and Joyce White

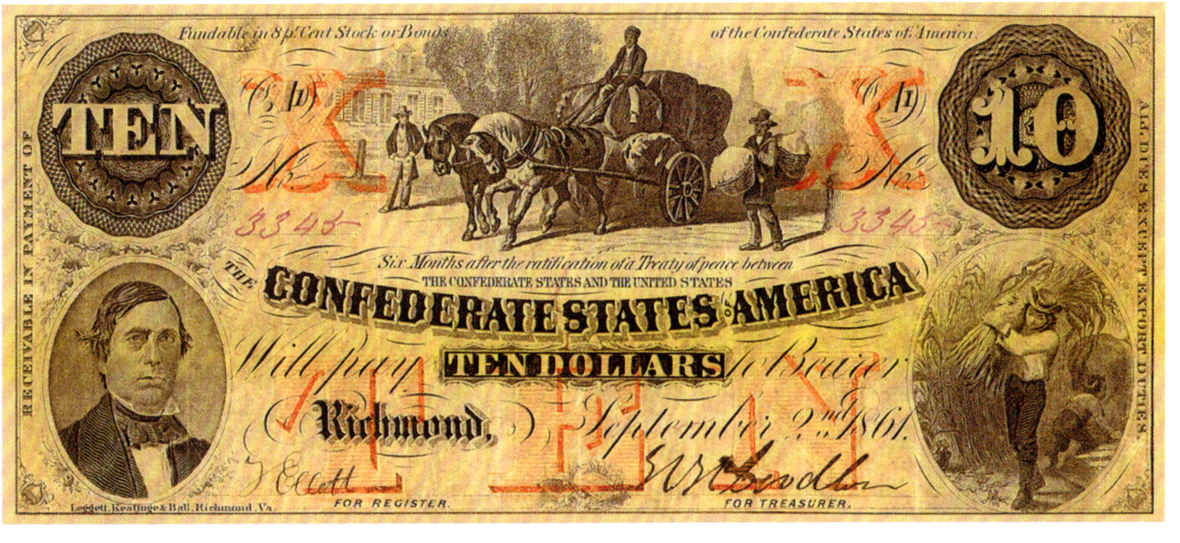

49 Slaves Moving Cotton

Collection of Avery Research Center Museum

50 Slave Driving Mules

Collection of Dr. Harold Rhodes III

51 Wagon Load of Cotton

Collection of Harriet McAdoo

52 Slaves and Cotton Bales

Collection of Christopher R. Wilkins

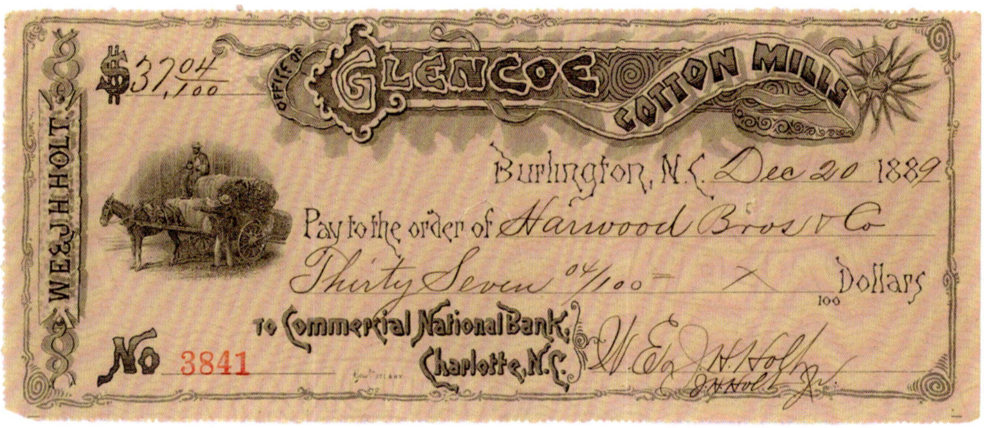

53 Slave Delivering Cotton

Collection of Agnes C. Powell, Esq.

54 Slaves with Cotton Cargo

Collection of Ann Perry

55 The Cotton Market

Collection of Dr. Harold Rhodes III

56 Slave Mule Team

Collection of Claudette Smith

57 Slave Going to the Docks

Collection of John W. Jones

58 Slaves Moving Barrels

Collection of Rev. Jesse Hawkins

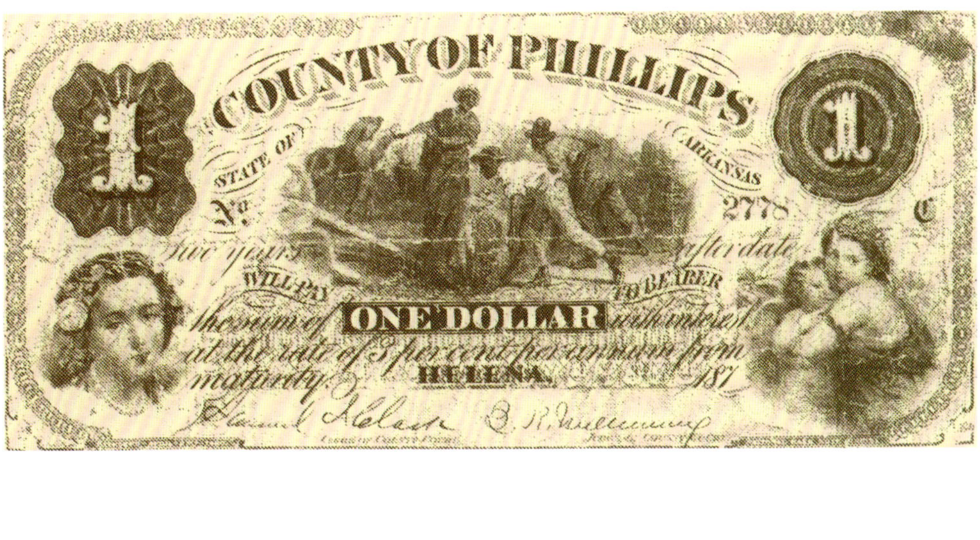

59 Slaves on the Levee

Collection of Melvin and Gislaine Johnson

60 Slave Dock Workers

Collection of Dr. Harold Rhodes III

61 Slave Dock Boys

Collection of Dr. Allan Rashford

62 Slaves Loading Ship I

Collection of Dr. Louis Hassell

63 Slaves Loading Ship II

Collection of Rev. Dr. Wayne D. Pokorny

64 Slaves Loading Ship III

Collection of Col. Carolyn White

65 Slaves Stacking Cotton

Collection of John Shefton

STOCKHOLDERS
NORTH CAROLINA.
RESPONSIBLE
Bank of Vanceyville
Will pay the bearer on demand
FOUR DOLLARS
Vanceyville
Cash.
Pres.

Factory Workers

Southerners also knew that if slavery could be transferred from the fields to the factories, slave owners could control the emerging industrial economy in America and the world. "Slave Factory Workers" is the only known image of slaves in an industrial setting, however. Southerners were worried that if slaves proved intelligent enough to operate a machine, it would be difficult to justify keeping them in bondage. In addition, the concept of industrial slavery was threatening to white wage laborers and the economic dominance of factory owners who had to pay for labor.

NORTH CAROLINA.
STOCKHOLDERS
RESPONSIBLE
4
Bank of Vanceyville
4
Will pay the bearer on demand
FOUR DOLLARS
Vanceyville
18
No.
A
Cash.
Pres.

66 Slave Factory Workers

Collection of Horace Felix

Propaganda

Images on Southern currencies circulating throughout the country were designed to reinforce Southern convictions about the legitimacy of enslaved labor and to convince Northerners of its beneficial nature for Africans. Images were increasingly characterized by smiling workers and well dressed blacks in happy scenes. Note the painful hypocrisy in portraying a happy mother and child within a system that routinely separated families and sold children.

67 Slave Boy

Collection of Ronald O. and Mittie R. Smith

68 Slave Mother and Child

Collection of Sybil Y. Parson

69 Arkansas Slave

Collection of Don Dogget

70 House Slave

Collection of Ann Perry

71 Slaves Taking a Swim

Collection of Al Miller

72 Slaves Nooning

Collection of Dr. Leon Lester and Sidra Freeman

73 Slave in Fancy Clothes

Collection of Rev. Dr. Wayne Pokorny

74 Slave Couple

Collection of Dr. Harold Rhodes III

75 Slave Riding Horse

Collection of Agnes C. Powell, Esq.

76 Montgomery Slave

Collection of Ruth Eagle

The Eastern Bank of Alabama
TEN DOLLARS
EUFAULA
American Bank Note Company
EUFAULA

Symbols of Legitimacy

Images of slavery were also connected with symbols of national legitimacy such as George Washington, himself a slaveholder, and the American flag. Notice how the artist paints the sky in "Slaves Unloading Cotton" to emphasize the connection which the engravers made between slavery and the American flag.

Sectional conflict over who would control the United States economy, Southern slave owners or Northern industrial interests, led to the Civil War.

77 Slave Carting Cotton

Collection of Dr. Harold Rhodes III

78 Slaves Unloading Cotton

Collection of Alphonso Brown

79 George Washington and Slave at Mount Vernon

Collection of Bernard Beal

80 Slave Feeding Horse

Collection of Rick and Beryl Strong

Legacy

Though the end of the Civil War abolished slavery, its destructive images of racism and discrimination prevailed, engraved on currencies in the South through a century of Jim Crow laws and segregation. As late as 1872, for example, an image of "happy" slaves picking cotton appeared with George Washington on a $50.00 revenue bond scrip issued by the State of South Carolina.

The image of Slaves on a note issued by the Atlantic and Gulf Railroad directly engages the issue of reparations in its testimony to how its present day progeny, the CSX Corporation, is beholden to the profits of slave labor. Other currencies in the exhibition provide similar evidence.

81 Slaves Picking Cotton

Collection of Dr. Harold Rhodes

COMMON STOCK

CERTIFICATE FOR LESS THAN 100 SHARES

Number 015382

Shares 15

TOBACCO PRODUCTS CORPORATION

INCORPORATED UNDER THE LAWS OF THE STATE OF VIRGINIA.

This is to Certify that Laidlaw & Co

is the owner of Fifteen full paid and non-assessable shares, of the par value of $100 each, of the COMMON STOCK of Tobacco Products Corporation, transferable in person or by attorney upon surrender of this certificate properly endorsed. A statement of the rights, privileges, preferences, restrictions and qualifications of the Preferred Stock, the Class A Stock and the Common Stock appears upon the back hereof, and this certificate and the shares of stock represented hereby are issued, received and held subject to all of the provisions of the Certificate of Incorporation and By-Laws of the Corporation, as amended (copies of which, as amended, are on file with the Transfer Agent) to all the provisions of which and of any further amendment to said Certificate of Incorporation and to said By-Laws the holder by acceptance hereof assents. This certificate [illegible] not valid until countersigned by the Transfer Agent and registered by the Registrar.

Witness the seal of the Corporation and the signatures of its duly authorized officers this JUN 26 1923

ASSISTANT SECRETARY.

VICE-PRESIDENT.

REGISTERED: THE CHASE NATIONAL BANK OF THE CITY OF NEW YORK, REGISTRAR.

ASSISTANT CASHIER

COUNTERSIGNED: GUARANTY TRUST COMPANY OF NEW YORK, TRANSFER AGENT.

ASSISTANT SECRETARY

82 Slaves Harvesting Tobacco

Collection of Barbara and Chuma Nwokike

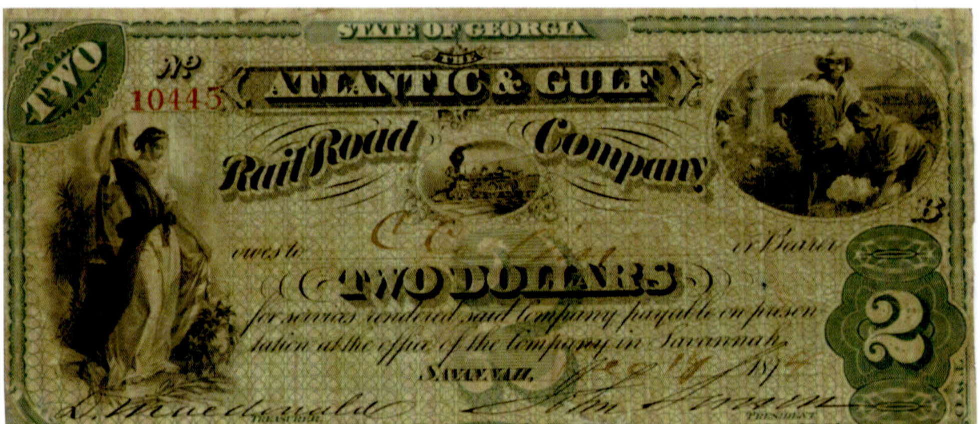

83 Georgia Slaves

Collection of Al Miller

Currency Listing

Scenes of American life depicting famous people, historical events, classical mythology and rural landscapes began to appear on notes in the early 1800s. Currency issuers, who wanted designs that would entice consumers to use their notes, selected images from proof notes provided by engravers. Some images were very popular, such as Slave Carrying Cotton which appeared on notes from at least 21 institutions.

This important iconography of slavery has been preserved by those individuals who were compelled to collect these historical documents. It is available today for scholars and citizens alike to study and learn about an institution and a people—both those who enslaved and those who were enslaved.

This section presents a sample of the currencies on which multiple images of individual engravings of slavery appeared.

STATE OF TENNESSEE.
FIVE
SHELBY COUNTY
4th SERIES. No. 8,230. for the year 1874.
This Certifies Shelby County is indebted to Selma, Marion and Memphis Rail Road, or bearer, the sum of
FIVE DOLLARS,
for Stock Subscription in said Road.
This Certificate is issued in pursuance of an order of the Quarterly Court at January Term 1871 ratified by the constitutional majority of the votes of the people of Shelby County, March 25th 1871, and receivable for special Tax levied by said Court to pay the same payable on demand out of the said special Tax, as soon as the same can be collected, and the whole to be paid twelve months after date.
Memphis Tenn. April 25th 1874.
5
Chairman of the County Court.

2
769.
TWO
Selma, Marion and Memphis
RAILROAD CO.
MARION, ALA. MARCH 1st 1871.
Pay to the Bearer
TWO DOLLARS
in Merchandise at their Store.
Treasurer
Countersigned
N. B. Forrest President.

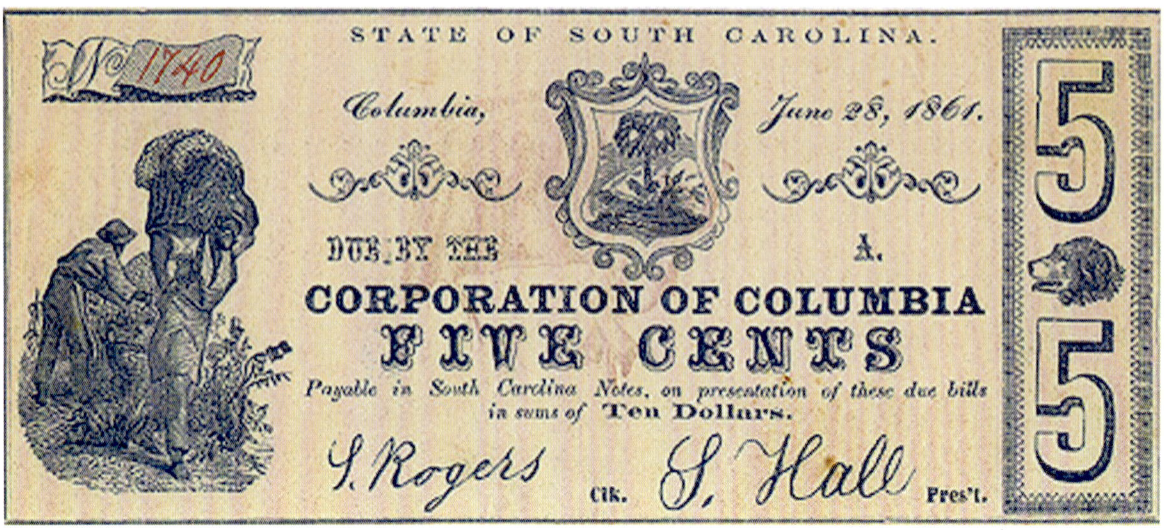
STATE OF SOUTH CAROLINA.
No 1740
Columbia, June 28, 1861.
DUE BY THE A.
CORPORATION OF COLUMBIA
FIVE CENTS
Payable in South Carolina Notes, on presentation of these due bills in sums of Ten Dollars.
S. Rogers Clk. S. Hall Pres't.
5
5

FIVE
A The STATE OF FLORIDA A
No.
Will pay FIVE DOLLARS to bearer
on Demand TALLAHASSEE January 1 1862
Contr.
Treas.
Hoyer & Ludwig Richmond Va
5

V
MACON, GEORGIA, MARCH 16, 1863.
THIS CERTIFIES THAT
A
FIVE DOLLARS
IN
C.S. TREASURY NOTES
HAVE BEEN DEPOSITED
IN THE
Macon Savings Bank.
PAYABLE TO THE HOLDER
In Confederate Treasury Notes.
Cashier
WITH FOUR PER CENT INTEREST AFTER THIRTY DAYS NOTICE
5

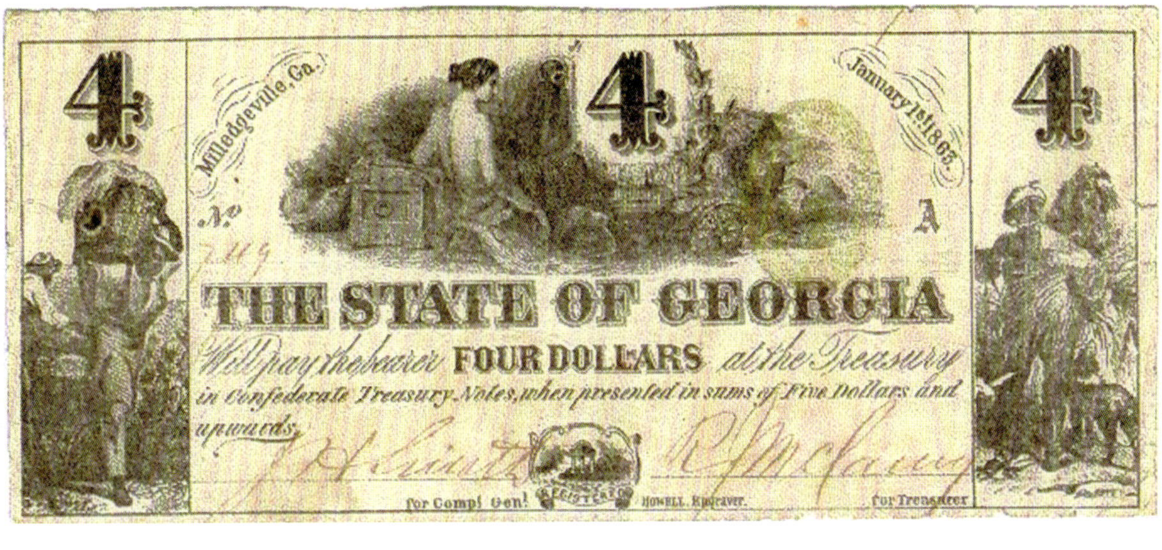
4
Milledgeville, Ga.
January 1st 1863
No
A
THE STATE OF GEORGIA
Will pay the bearer FOUR DOLLARS at the Treasury
in Confederate Treasury Notes, when presented in sums of Five Dollars and upwards.
For Compt Genl.
HOWELL, Engraver.
For Treasurer
REGISTERED

V
MACON, GEORGIA, MARCH 16, 1865.
5
THIS CERTIFIES THAT
A
FIVE DOLLARS
IN
C.S. TREASURY NOTES
HAVE BEEN DEPOSITED
IN THE
Macon Savings Bank.
PAYABLE TO THE HOLDER
In Confederate Treasury Notes

2
EXCHANGE BANK
2
TWO
OF THE STATE OF GEORGIA
TWO DOLLARS
GRIFFIN
Cash.
Pres.

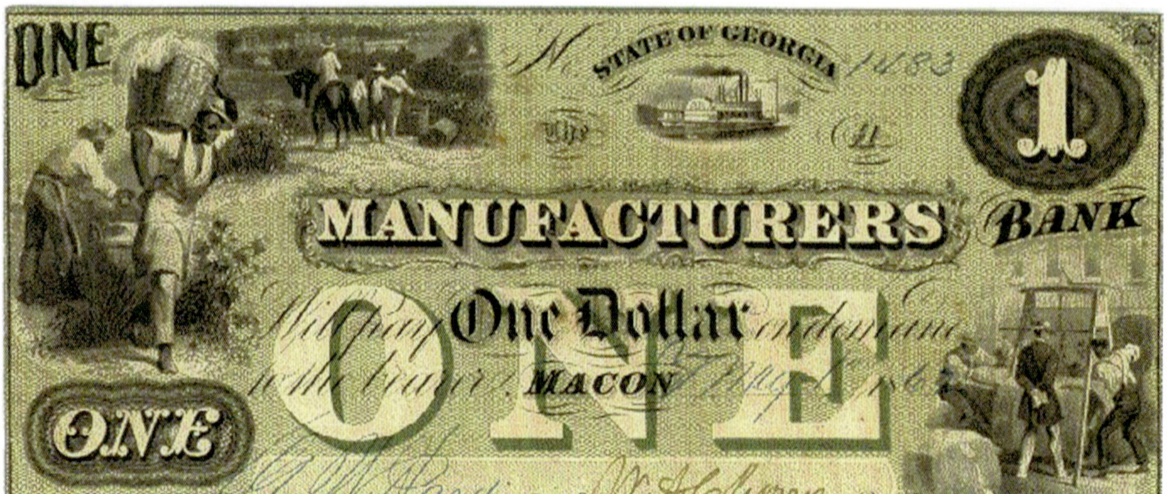
ONE
STATE OF GEORGIA
1
MANUFACTURERS
BANK
One Dollar
MACON
ONE
ONE
Cash.
Pres.

2
STATE OF GEORGIA
THE BANK OF MORGAN
TWO DOLLARS
ON DEMAND
TWO
Cash.
Pres.

50
THE TRADERS BANK
OF THE CITY OF RICHMOND
Will Pay
TO BEARER
ON DEMAND
No.
FIFTY DOLLARS
RICHMOND
VIRGINIA
18
Cash.
Pres.
STOCKHOLDERS RESPONSIBLE

1
TIMBER CUTTER'S BANK
ONE DOLLAR
ON DEMAND
SAVANNAH,
Cash.
Pres.
GEORGIA

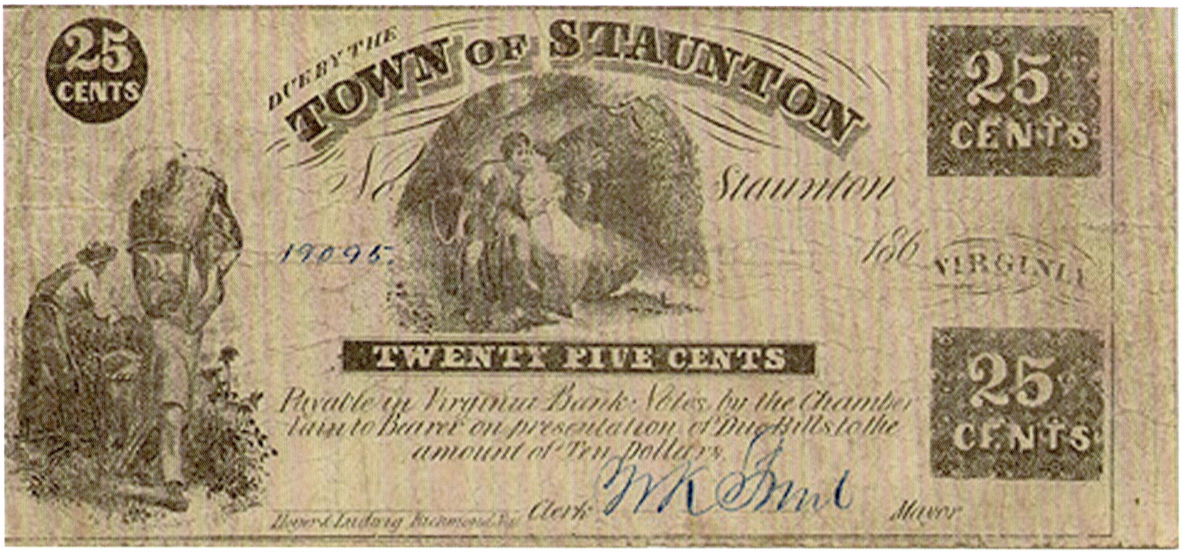
25 CENTS
DUE BY THE
TOWN OF STAUNTON
No.
Staunton
186
VIRGINIA
TWENTY FIVE CENTS
Payable in Virginia Bank Notes by the Chamberlain to Bearer on presentation of Due Bills to the amount of Ten Dollars.
Clerk
Mayor
25 CENTS
25 CENTS

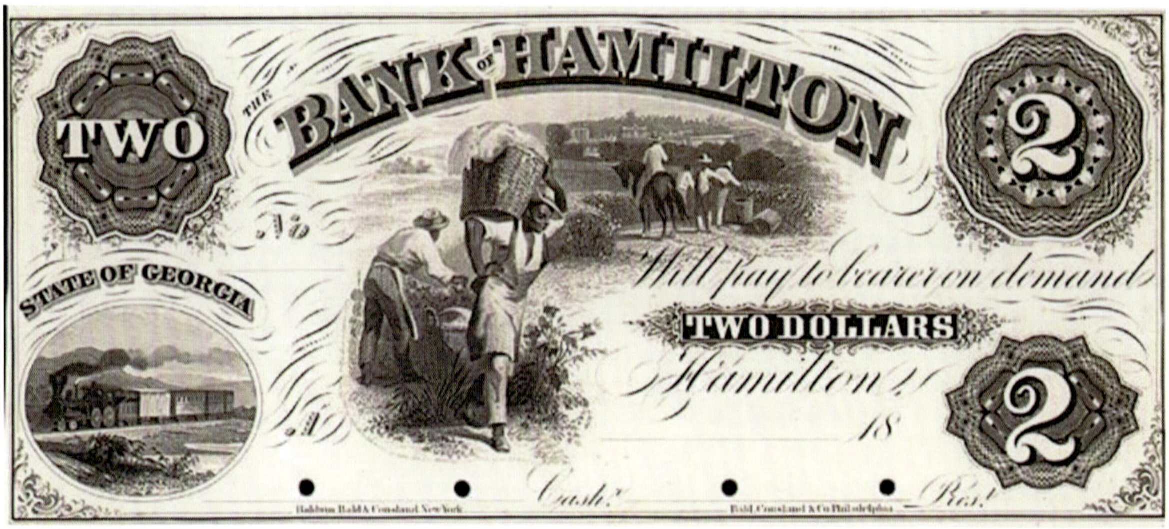
TWO
THE BANK OF HAMILTON
STATE OF GEORGIA
2
Will pay to bearer on demand
TWO DOLLARS
Hamilton
18
Cash.r
Pres.t
2

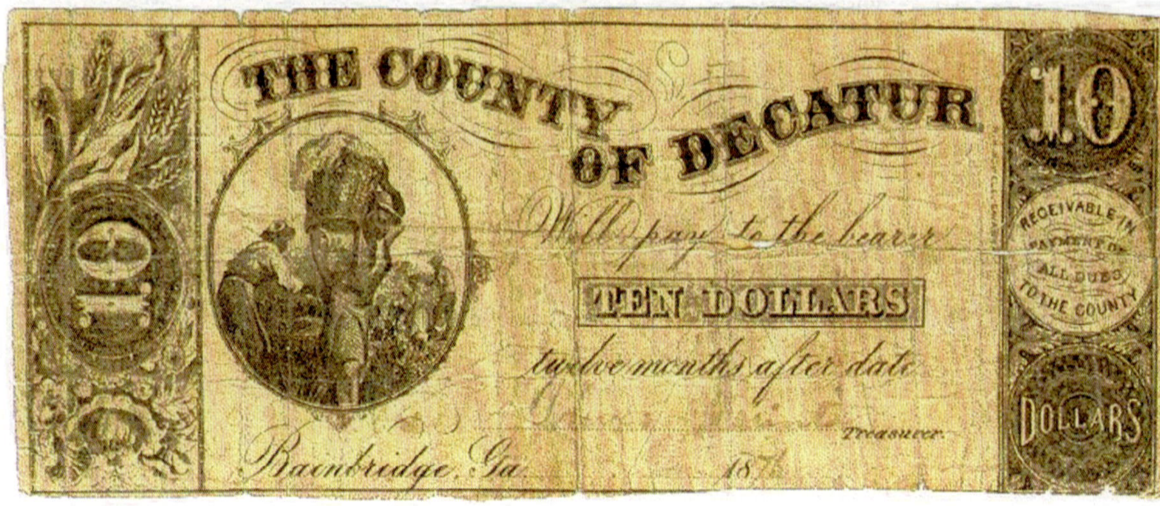
THE COUNTY OF DECATUR
Will pay to the bearer
TEN DOLLARS
twelve months after date
Treasurer.
Bainbridge, Ga.
187
10
RECEIVABLE IN PAYMENT OF ALL DUES TO THE COUNTY
DOLLARS

BANK OF GREENSBOROUGH
2
TWO
Will Pay
TO BEARER
DOLLARS
ON DEMAND
Greensborough
Cash.
Pres.

STATE OF
GEORGIA
BANK OF ATHENS
10
Will Pay
TO BEARER
ON DEMAND
TEN DOLLARS
ATHENS
Cash.
Pres.

STATE OF
GEORGIA
1
B
THE BANK OF COMMERCE
ONE
ONE DOLLAR
ON DEMAND
Cash.
Pres.

Montgomery Feb 22nd 1861.
THE COUNTY OF MONTGOMERY
ALABAMA
No 1335
Five Dollars
American Bank Note Co. New York

State of Georgia.
THE MANUFACTURERS BANK
ON DEMAND
TWENTY DOLLARS
CASH.
PRES.
American Bank Note Company

TWENTY
20
THE MERCHANTS & PLANTERS BANK in the City OF AUGUSTA
Promises to pay or bearer on demand
TWENTY dollars
AUGUSTA GEO.
Cash.
Pres.

STATE OF
GEORGIA
THE BANK OF COLUMBUS
ONE
1
Will Pay
ONE DOLLAR
ON DEMAND

TEN
EXCHANGE BANK
HELENA, ARK.
10
Pay
on demand
TEN DOLLARS
or Bearer.

ALABAMA
The Bank of Selma
10
Will pay
TEN DOLLARS
to bearer
on demand
SELMA
Secured by the Pledge of Public Stocks

10
STATE OF
NORTH CAROLINA
THE
MINERS & PLANTERS BANK
WILL PAY
on demand
to the bearer
Ten Dollars
TEN
MURPHY
Cash.
Pres.
Stockholders individually liable

MASSACHUSETTS
ONE
1
Will pay
Bearer
ONE DOLLAR
ON DEMAND
Cash.
Pres.

STATE OF GEORGIA
ONE
1
THE
SOUTHERN BANK
Will pay
Bearer
ONE DOLLAR
ON DEMAND
Cash.
Pres.

STATE OF
ALABAMA.
2
TWO
No.
A
CENTRAL BANK
OF ALABAMA,
Will pay TWO DOLLARS to the bearer
on demand. MONTGOMERY,
Cash.

B
10
Eastern Bank of Alabama
TEN
Will pay TEN DOLLARS on demand
to the bearer. EUFAULA 18
Cash.
Pres.

SOUTHERN BANK
50
THE
OF
No. 2451
GEORGIA.
Will pay FIFTY DOLLARS to the bearer on demand
BAINBRIDGE.
April 10, 1849.
FIFTY
Cash.
Prest.

TALLAHASSEE, March 1st 1864.
No.
THE STATE OF FLORIDA
Will pay to the bearer on demand
TEN DOLLARS
Treasurer
Governor

Tallahassee, March 1st 1863.
ONE
THE STATE OF FLORIDA
Will pay to the bearer on demand
ONE DOLLAR
Treasurer
Governor

MISSISSIPPI
TREASURY NOTE
100
JACKSON, MISS:
THE STATE OF MISSISSIPPI
One Hundred Dollars
Auditor
Treasurer

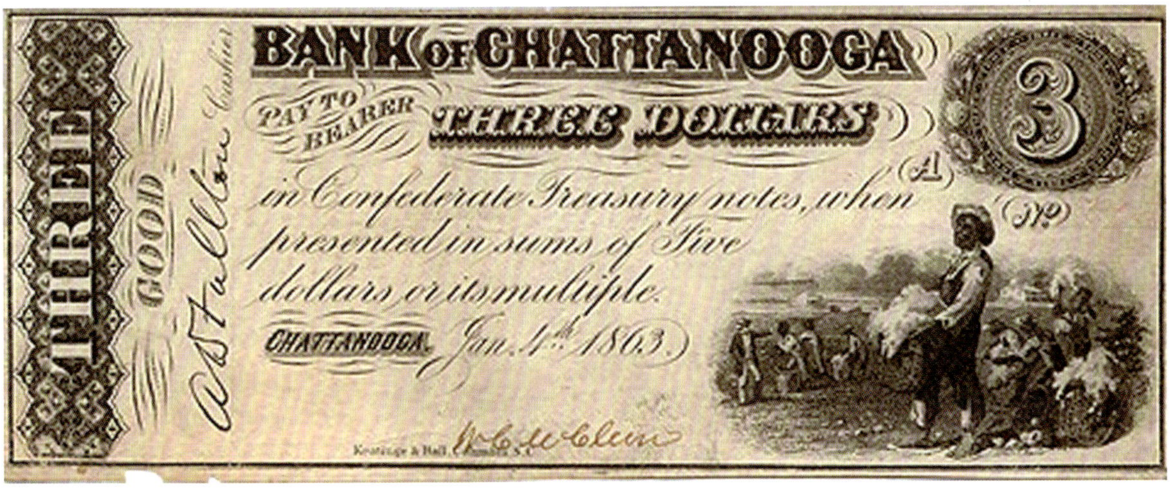
BANK OF CHATTANOOGA
PAY TO BEARER THREE DOLLARS
in Confederate Treasury notes, when presented in sums of Five dollars or its multiple.
CHATTANOOGA, Jan. 1st 1863
THREE
GOOD
3

REQUISITION FOR
MISSOURI DEFENCE BONDS,
On demand the Fund Commissioners of the
STATE OF MISSOURI
Will pay to the order of the
FIFTY Dollars in Missouri Defence Bonds
50

THIS CERTIFIES THAT THERE HAS BEEN DEPOSITED IN THE
GEORGIA SAVINGS BANK
IN CONFEDERATE TREASURY NOTES
TWENTY DOLLARS
Payable to the Bearer at the option of the Bank in confederate Treasury or current bank notes
MACON, Ga
June 15th 1862
20
Cash'r

THE AUGUSTA INSURANCE & BANKING Co.
GEORGIA
10
TEN DOLLARS
No. 1391 B
Cash
Pres
American Bank Note Company

MISSISSIPPI
TREASURY NOTE
10
10
JACKSON, MISS.
THE STATE OF MISSISSIPPI
TEN DOLLARS
Auditor
Treasurer
American Bank Note Co. N.Y. & N.O.

ONE HUNDRED
THE FARMERS & MECHANICS
BANK
WILL PAY
ON DEMAND
ONE HUNDRED DOLLARS
No. 927
No. 927
100
100
SAVANNAH,
STATE OF GEORGIA
100
HUNDRED
Cashier
President
American Bank Note Company

State of Georgia
THE Bank OF Commerce
50
50
Will pay FIFTY DOLLARS to bearer
on demand SAVANNAH
FIFTY
Cashr
Presr
No 186

STATE OF
GEORGIA
THE TIMBER CUTTER'S BANK
2
2
TO BEARER
ON DEMAND
TWO DOLLARS
SAVANNAH
Cash
Pres

NORTH CAROLINA
THE BANK OF WADESBOROUGH
4
4
Will pay FOUR DOLLARS to bearer
on demand
WADESBOROUGH
No
FOUR
FOUR
Cashr
Presr

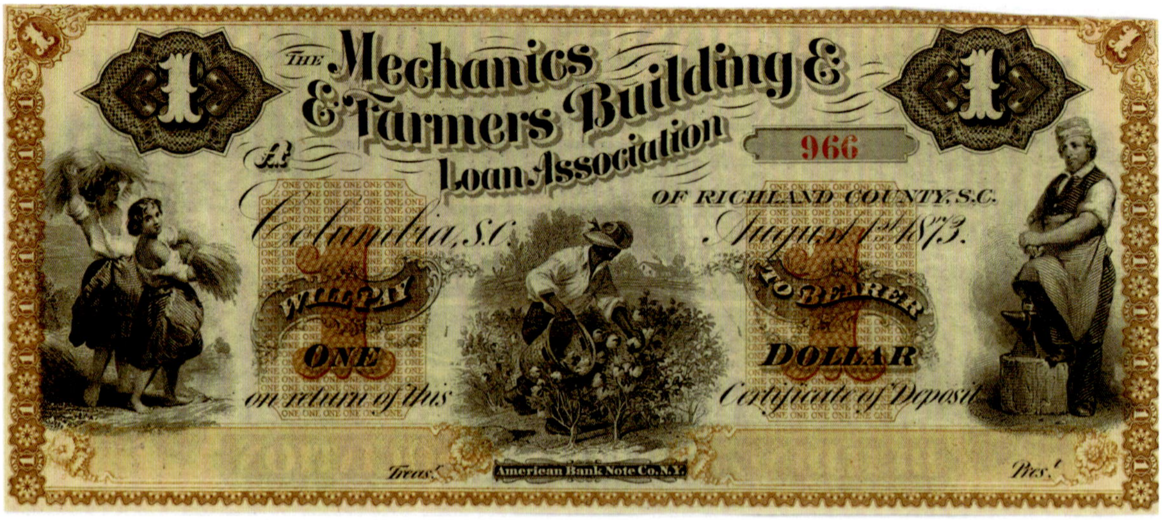
THE Mechanics & Farmers Building & Loan Association
OF RICHLAND COUNTY, S.C.
966
Columbia, S.C. August 1st 1873.
WILL PAY ONE
TO BEARER DOLLAR
on return of this Certificate of Deposit
Treas.
Pres.
American Bank Note Co. N.Y.

FIVE
Nashville, May 1st 1875.
No. 4094
PAYABLE WARRANT.
Treasury of the
STATE OF TENNESSEE
PAY TO
FIVE DOLLARS

STATE OF VIRGINIA
No.
THE TRADERS BANK OF THE CITY OF RICHMOND
TWENTY
Will pay Dollars
to bearer on demand
Twenty Twenty
STOCKHOLDERS RESPONSIBLE
RICHMOND 18
Cash.
Pres.
TWENTY DOLLARS

STATE OF
GEORGIA
TEN
10
MECHANICS SAVINGS BANK
OF SAVANNAH
TEN DOLLARS
TEN

MISSISSIPPI
TREASURY NOTE
50
STATE OF MISSISSIPPI
FIFTY DOLLARS
JACKSON, MISS.
American Bank Note Co. N.Y. & N.O.

REVENUE
BOND SCRIP
FIVE
5
4276
STATE OF SOUTH CAROLINA
FIVE DOLLARS
STATE TREASURER

100
100
CANAL BANK
The New Orleans Canal & Banking Company
Promises to pay One Hundred dollars to the bearer
on demand New Orleans, 18
Cash.
Pres.

ONE
NORFOLK
1
1
THE EXCHANGE BANK
OF VIRGINIA
Will pay One Dollar on demand to
bearer at its Banking House in Norfolk
Cash.
Pres.

20
20
THE
BANK SOUTH CAROLINA
TWENTY DOLLARS
CHARLESTON
TWENTY
Cash.
Pres.
TWENTY TWENTY TWENTY

MISSISSIPPI
TREASURY NOTE
20
20
THE STATE OF MISSISSIPPI
TWENTY DOLLARS
JACKSON, MISS.
Auditor
Treasurer
American Bank Note Co. N.Y. & N.O.

STATE OF
GEORGIA
XX
20
BANK OF COLUMBUS
TWENTY
TWENTY DOLLARS
ON DEMAND.
XX
Cash.
Pres.

No 1346
5
5
THE MISSISSIPPI
& ALABAMA
RAIL-ROAD COMPANY
Promises to pay FIVE dollars on demand
or bearer. Brandon Miss.
Cash.
Pres.
5
5
Draper, Toppan, Longacre & Co. Phil. & NY

5
5
SOUTHERN BANK KENTUCKY
Will pay FIVE DOLLARS at their Bank
in to the bearer on demand.
RUSSELLVILLE
Cash.
5
5

FIVE
THE STATE of ALABAMA.
RECEIVABLE IN PAYMENT OF
ALL TAXES AND PUBLIC DUES
5
No
Will pay FIVE DOLLARS to Bearer
Redeemable in CONFEDERATE TREASURY NOTES or in FIVE PER CENT. COUPON BONDS of the State, at the option of the State.

No 3038
10
10
THE
CENTRAL BANK OF VIRGINIA
Will pay TEN DOLLARS to Bearer
on demand.
STAUNTON
Cash.
Pres.
American Bank Note Company
X

List of Paintings

All measurements are (height) x (width) in inches

Arranged alphabetically

Contributors

Gretchen Barbatsis is a Professor of Telecommunication at Michigan State University and serves as Consulting Faculty in the African Studies Center, the Center for Advanced International Development and the Women and International Development Program. Her scholarly and creative work focuses on instructional media design and visual communication. She has directed development communication projects in Africa as well as inner city communities in the United States.

Richard G. Doty is a Curator of American history at the Smithsonian Institution,Washington, DC. A recipient of the Millennium Medal of the Royal Numismatic Society, he has lectured throughout the world on virtually all aspects of numismatics. His contributions include scholarship on obsolete bank notes and paper money of the Confederate States of America, and recent books include *America's Money-America's Story* and *Money of the World*. He has also written numerous radio scripts and an award winning CD, *The Riches of Coins*.

Curtis Franks is the Director of Museum Education and Exhibits at the Avery Research Center for African American History and Culture at the College of Charleston, where he has served as Curator of numerous exhibitions related to the African and African American experience in South Carolina. His scholarship in African American history, which emphasizes oral history methodology, is enriched by his lifelong experience as a bibliophile and collector of African and African American material and artifacts.

Wilmont A. Fraser is a Professor of African American Studies, retired from Cheyney University Pennsylvania. He is an historian and folklorist of African American culture. He is the co-author of *To Be or Not...to Bop— Memoirs of Dizzy Gillespie.*

Jack McCray is with The Post and Courier of Charleston, SC, the South's oldest daily newspaper, as an Arts and Culture writer, a book reviewer and a copywriter. His freelance writing interests include jazz music as well as American and African American history. He has contributed to *Jazz Times, Lowcountry Heritage Society,* and the magazine of the South Carolina Historical Society, *Carologue.*

Donald West is an Instructor of History, Humanities and Government at Trident Technical College of Charleston where he teaches African American and United States history. His scholarly interests include African American history, archival administration and museum studies. He is a contributing member of the Association for the Study of African American History.

About the Artist

John W. Jones, a slave descendant was born and raised in Columbia, SC. He has been a freelance artist and illustrator for more than twenty years.

Jones explores life through art. This multi-talented artist uses oils, acrylics and watercolors for his painting. Striving for detail in light and reflection, he meticulously draws each painting first and then layers it with color, resulting in very realistic interpretations of everyday life and landscapes, as well as historical insights into our past.

Jones' work is in several private and public collections including the Charleston Metro Chamber of Commerce, the City of Charleston, and the College of Charleston.

Published works in the past three years, include covers of the Charleston Area Visitors Guide and the Farmers' Market. Jones' work received merit awards in the Piccolo Spoleto Outdoor Art Show in 1998 and 1999.

His paintings are available at the Rita Smith Gallery in Columbia, SC and Chuma Gullah Galley in Charleston, SC